THE SNIPPETS OF A LIFE

From Depressed Victim to Proud Woman

An Autobiography of

Innocence
Betrayal
Humiliation
Guilt
Confusion
Shame
Pain
Fear
Hopelessness

Recovery
Forgiveness
Happiness

Still working on it…

Kirsten Gershon

The Snippets of a Life

Editor's Note: A sincere effort was made by this editor to maintain Ms. Gershon's unique voice throughout this book. English is not her original language. Certain grammatical allowances or freedoms were employed to remain authentic with the author's voice. Joy B. Leffler

PUBLISHING HISTORY
First Edition 2017

COVER DESIGN
Julie Ray Creative LLC
Incorporating original art by
Dan Gershon

Technical and moral support Cindy Cooper

ISBN 10: 0998824712
ISBN 13: 9780998824710

Web Page: thesnippetsofalife.com

TABLE OF CONTENTS

PREFACE

I am writing this book from a healing point of view and not in any real chronological order. I may write about one subject for a while, skip it and come back to it, as my healing and thinking change over time.

My intention is to write my life story exactly the way I remember it. Sometimes my memories take me to unpleasant places. I am not out to hurt anyone or to be vengeful. I am just telling it all as it feels when I look inward and meet my sad inner children. I know that siblings growing up and living in the same family can remember things in a very different way. I can only be truthful to my own feelings and memories.

I have worked for decades to change my thinking and behavior from misunderstood victim to proud woman—from only reacting, to actually thinking and analyzing—from believing I was a second-class citizen, to knowing that I have rights to my own life and feelings. I have been hiding the real me and my childhood for way too long and it's time to come out of the bush.

Recently, I became an American citizen. This change in my life prompted me to begin to write. I sat down and wrote about how it felt to become a new American citizen. It was a life-changing experience for me—the whole reason this book got started in the first place.

Twenty years ago, I read it would be a helpful tool to write your life in third person…as a fairytale. The writing in third person would make it less threatening. I never wrote the fairytale. Shortly after becoming an American, I felt the urge to do just that. I sat in a comfy chair, pen in hand and began writing. The whole fairytale section was done in less than 30 minutes. I knew I could write but had never really trusted my ability before. I had always listened to and believed my parent's judgment of me. Whatever I tried, they would diminish it and I would never try again. "So, you think you are a writer or a painter? So, you think that you can do anything you want to do?" I learned to fear everything and these same fears are with me today. I have never fully recovered from these old judgments. To write this book is a testament to my newfound courage.

WHY WRITE A BOOK LIKE THIS?

To be brutally honest, it isn't easy. There are a lot of fears involved with letting it all out. I am convinced that we need to learn to talk about the sad stuff. If we don't, we are robots without feelings. Our feelings can only be pushed away to a certain point before we begin to fall apart. Our emotions are there for a reason. Our inner soul is as important as the rest of us. Why don't we listen when it tries to tell us that we are on the wrong track? We sometimes hear the little voices from the core, but we ignore them.

Professionals usually write healing stories that include the suffering and crazy thoughts of unnamed clients. We rarely hear from the person who goes through the crying and the hard work of healing. As we grow up, we do not learn to dare to see, feel, or talk about our raw, honest emotions. I am sure that some parents can create a healthy emotional life for themselves and their children. But, in my understanding, we live in a world where we are taught to run away from anything unpleasant. It's as if we were promised happiness and freedom from problems for all our lives. This kind of thinking can only set us up for life-long failure and sadness. *Don't ever air your sad, angry or unpleasant thoughts. Go through life with a phony smile and, of course, always have the perfect body, hair, house, and car.* Everyone is gorgeous and fabulous on TV or in magazines. No one seems to have any problems whatsoever.

How can we live up to all these false expectations—not to mention the cost of being perfect? It is not possible, and it wears us down. Unfortunately, we let the show go on for way too long or until we are burned out. Then, after years of being the perfect person and surrounded by the perfect friends and neighbors, we wonder where to go with the sad stuff. We push it farther and farther away with hectic lifestyles, overwork, food, drugs, facelifts, shopping and hundreds of other distractions. The thought that somebody would think less of us if we dared open up is difficult to get past. What will make you happy? Will it be Mr. Right or a prince on the white horse? How about moving to another country, having a baby or having enough money? Will these make you happy?

I have news for you. I have tried all of these. The inner turmoil follows you around. No circumstance can really heal you unless you are willing to look at yourself. Happiness and healing begin from within and not from the outside world. Our soul needs honesty and a good cry every once in a while. Get off the computer for a while and get to know the wonderful feeling of really connecting with another human being. My hope is to share my story so that others might begin to open up to *their* truth. I believe that shared problems are halved and lead you to the path of happiness.

UPON BECOMING AN AMERICAN CITIZEN

January 8, 2016

I just became an American citizen and went to a very touching ceremony. The new citizens came from many different countries and various backgrounds, and we were all happy and proud to become Americans. Some new Americans came from very poor countries and had gone through terrible hardships; others were more fortunate. Together on that day, we became the same—the new hopeful citizens of a country full of immigrants who all see this country as different, aspiring and bold. A real game changer.

I personally have always looked at Americans as a proud and a daring people. You are allowed to think, say and become whoever you wish to be. The class system and the unwritten rules of so many other countries don't seem to work here. If you want to walk down Main Street in a funny suit and a ridiculous hat while singing, no one will stop you or judge you. They will only look at you as a different kind of person, someone to smile at or with…but not as a lesser human being. This is what is so freeing about America. *Go do with your life as you see fit*…the right to pursue happiness. What a concept! No one else but you can decide what will make you happy. It's a freedom, and it comes with responsibilities. You and only you can make it happen.

The judge who spoke at the ceremony told all of us that there are two very important responsibilities associated with becoming American. Firstly, get involved, vote and get your voice heard. Secondly, be strong and use your talents to make this country better. Whatever talent it is, use it; we can't all be Einstein. Every human being has something to give. To me, these were very strong words. After all, I grew up in Denmark in a family where you try not to stand out, not to be too loud, not to be seen too much. "*Do not think you are better than anybody else. Who do you think you are? Don't think that you can amount to anything.*" The judge's words sparked new thoughts in my brain. Maybe I am unique. Maybe I do have some kind of talents. Maybe I can add something to this big country. What a heartwarming thought. Already, on this first day as an American, I am greeted with so much more love, hope and trust in me as a person—more than I received in all my 57 years. *You are good enough. You might even add to this country.* The sky is the limit. WOW!

I have wanted to write my life story for a long time, but I never had the courage or trust in my own abilities. After hearing the judge say, "Go out there and do what you do. Nothing is wrong. You are an American now." It has only been three weeks since then, and I now begin to write. I am going to write in English, even if it comes out a little childish at times. This is who I am in my new country with nothing to be ashamed of…just another American citizen with a unique life story.

A REAL-LIFE FAIRYTALE

Once upon a time, there was a little girl. She lived in a very poor housing project with her parents and her siblings. Almost all of the other houses in her country were big and beautiful. The girl was very sad because the father was cruel and sarcastic and always made fun of her. He also loved to humiliate her in front of others. He was not a good dad, and the little girl wanted to run away. Where to go? How to get food? How to live? The little girl tried very hard to please her father, but he had no patience with her and didn't care.

The little girl also had a mother, and the little girl loved her so much; but, the mother had secrets, and the girl became involved in these secrets, which were just as scary as her dad's cruelty. The little girl didn't know that she was tricked into doing things that weren't good. These things couldn't be felt or told—or even whispered. The mother was scared of life as well as the father. The mother saw trolls everywhere. She taught the girl that the world is a dangerous place, filled with frightening people. "*All men are terrible.*" The little girl and the mother were very snug together—against all those trolls. The little girl learned that to be a good friend of the mother came with a heavy price. The little girl had to become the mother's confidant and caregiver. The little girl became her mother's mother and her sexual partner. The little girl had to keep all this to herself. Secrets were never revealed, or the mother's love would stop. The whole world would think that the little girl was just a little, perverted liar.

The mother had super low self-esteem and felt that she was unworthy of anything and *less than* everybody else—stupid and ugly. The little girl was taught that part of her devotion to the mother was to stay forever stupid, poor and unworthy. The little girl wanted so badly to save her mother and would do whatever it took to do so. She had no chance. She couldn't say or even feel, "Stop—I am being exploited and abused." She thought she was doing the right thing.

She did not learn to live a normal life and had a very hard time with all the beautiful, first-class people out there in the world. The girl had a hard time with school and friendships. The holding of all the secrets became a full-time job, and the girl began to have headaches and to be sick a lot. The mother loved it when the little girl was sick, and she couldn't go to school. Then the mother had the little girl to herself. They could be intimate girlfriends, just the way the mother wanted them to be. They were creating the lie that the whole world was against them. We will always be the lowest in everything, but we have each other's back. The mother hoped the child would look after her for the rest of her life. Somewhere deep inside the little girl knew things weren't so good.

On most days, the little girl tried to stay outside as long as possible and maybe not come inside until bedtime. She always tried to be nice and to please everybody. When the little girl became a teenager, she stayed away even more. Climbing up the staircase to the apartment became a heavy burden; the girl had learned that she had to be what her parents wanted her to be. She wasn't allowed to be herself or have any wishes and ambitions. She was no longer aware of her own thoughts anyway. The poor girl—now young women—had just become a sad extension of her mother. The girl was afraid of everything—poor in a rich neighborhood and stupid amongst her smart peers. And the secrets kept piling up. One day she thought that she didn't even deserve food; she became very skinny. *See world…how little I need.* She had no wants and needs at all. Now she was the perfect daughter but totally dead inside.

Her peers went into life with good educations and somehow knew how to live and get ahead. The young woman married the wrong man, and she had a child very young.

One morning, angels came to her, and they told her that a better life was ahead if she wanted it, but first many obstacles were laid out for her. If she could get through these, while working and caring for her child, they promised the world would be a better place for her. *Well! My life can't get much worse.* She cried and hoped at the same time. Yes, the obstacles were many and lasted for years: a divorce, a long depression, and additional education. Now, she was feeling her loneliness. Then she slowly began to remember that little girl she once was. She was seeing the neglect and acknowledging the abuse. One day she realized that keeping secrets made her sick. She had to do something drastic to get out of this mess.

The angels kept their promises. She met a very nice man from a foreign country. She was ready to begin to trust herself, and she didn't listen when her parents told her that life in a foreign country was very scary and dangerous. Her prince loved her, and her son and they lived happily ever after…

Now the healing could begin.

WHAT IS THE MATTER WITH ME?

The ending of the fairy tale makes it sound like everything was now just smooth sailing but many years and bumpy roads lie ahead. Many memories and sad stories needed to be uncovered—told and retold before the "real me" could begin to emerge. The angels have been with me, but they did not do the hard work or shed the tears of pain for me. They were and still are there for me when I need a shoulder or when there is no one in the world to go to with my truth. What would people think if they really knew my story and me? I thought for many years that I was a second-class person and had no rights, not even to my own feelings. *My feelings are wrong.* Everything was my own stupid fault, and no one in the world would believe a word I said. My parents had really put out that trap for me, and I stepped into it. If I am the liar, then the truth can't hurt them.

My new life in Switzerland, as wonderful as it sounded, became the next staircase in my quest to find myself. My new husband traveled an awful lot, and my son went to school. I had a lot of time to think. Again, I felt very lonely—a recurring theme in my life. I stood out and didn't feel as though I could fit in at all. On top of all this, I had to learn to speak French and get to know a different culture.

There was something fundamental that I didn't understand. It wasn't about the new culture. What was it? In my new life, behind my facade of smiles, the same insecurities about my own value and my shame were just under the surface. I was always looking for clues as to what I was doing wrong. My everyday life was a lot less stressed than it used to be. Nonetheless, it was not an easy task to move to a foreign country with a language that I didn't understand. I struggled for years with the French language. It was also hard to see my son missing his friends and everything he knew back in Denmark. We had some hard years ahead of us— learning it all.

In my new marriage, I didn't have to work, and I didn't have to worry about money all the time. My husband was nice. My son liked his new school. The two of them became great friends. So why was

I afraid and still felt second-class? It wouldn't have mattered to which country I had moved. It was not a geographic problem; it was something inside me.

It was as if I was not allowed to be happy, successful or just like every other human being. I knew that a lot of people were a lot worse off than I was. I think a lot of us who raised ourselves became very hard parents and we had very little patience with ourselves. When you have to raise yourself and receive very little guidance and few or wrong role models, something happens in the brain and in the understanding of the world. I call this inner turmoil *The Soup.* For me, the world became a dangerous, unsafe, lonely and shame-filled place with nowhere to hide. I had the feeling that everybody, especially my mother, could read my mind and that I would always come out bad, wrong or less-than. All my life I feared everything and everybody. When life is so stressed, it is hard to concentrate in school and answer questions from teachers, parents or other adults. I took this stress with me to Switzerland and, for many years, my thinking patterns were the same as when I was a child.

WARPED THINKING

I would always try to figure out what would be the right answer to questions or the answers that would make me look less stupid. This was my misunderstanding and warped thinking. Sometimes I could hardly hear the questions. While thinking of the answer, my heart would start to pump, my cheeks would redden, and I would disappear in shame—a collapse of my soul. The simplest of questions could make me lose myself. I thought that there was only one right answer and that I had to come up with it in an instant. I thought that everybody knew the answer; they knew everything, and I didn't. I had to do everything possible to avoid detection. It was very hard for me to admit that I didn't know something and this put me in difficult situations. I didn't know how to just *be me* and *trust myself.* It never occurred to me that I could say things like, "I don't know" or "Let me think about it for a while." I had so misunderstood everything, and it took years and years to begin to figure it out.

I think I need to explain *The Soup* a little better. It's almost impossible to get out of *The Soup*. I didn't even know I was in it. *The Soup*, a learned way of being or thinking, prevented me from believing that I was a normal human being like everybody else. I couldn't see that the whole second-class thing wasn't real. I had been indoctrinated to feel and think in certain ways. I had no idea that I had voices and choices; therefore, I remained in *The Soup* for many years—a life lived without a manual or a rulebook. Low self-esteem prevented me from thinking for myself. I certainly didn't think I deserved any better. *Who do you think you are? You think you are better than your parents or your peers? Don't ever think you are smart and will amount to anything. The Soup* was negative and degrading. And what made *My Soup* so difficult to see? It had many different ingredients.

Lately, I have begun to think of *The Soup* as baking a cake. The first and biggest ingredient is fear, add to it almost the same amount of shame and sadness, a good portion of loneliness along with some feelings of less-than-others and a dash of hopelessness. Mix it all together in a bowl full of abuse. Bake well for many years, and the cake will taste absolutely awful.

The Soup is a learned way of thinking and a misunderstanding of what it means to be a person. When you live in *The Soup*, you do not know that life can look any other way. You believe you deserve it. You can try to better yourself and your life and try to take away one spoonful of *The Soup* at a time. Maybe *The Soup* gets a little better, but it is still with you. Friends and family don't like you when you act differently from them. I tried unloading *The Soup*, but the environment and the people around me wanted to heap more onto me. It was an endless and fatiguing process. Now on top of everything else was this enormous burden—weighing me down and wearing me out. "Kirsten could just work harder and pull herself together" or "If Kirsten would just stop being so negative..." I constantly felt like there was something I didn't know. *What is it that I can't figure out about life?* My brain was so stressed out that everyday small chores become mountains. *Hurry up and don't be seen. Don't make any mistakes or the world will humiliate me just as my dad did.*

The world did use and abuse me in many ways. I hadn't learned about boundaries or how to be safe around people. I didn't see the warning signs and remained in bad situations way too long. I attracted the wrong people and, when they treated me badly, I just took it. It was easy to be mistreated and stepped upon; I was already down. People around me would say, "You are too sensitive. You can't take a joke or suck it up." I heard these lines a lot. I know for a fact that it is not only children who bully but also adults. Many times, when I thought I had found a friend, I was to be hurt one more time. In workplaces as in schoolyards, the ones who struggled the hardest were the ones who got the biggest beatings—emotionally or otherwise. *Where is the compassion in this world?*

The Soup also interfered with my working life as a young adult. I was a good worker; my work was always done, but I always lost my jobs. I was never unemployed for long periods of time, but I couldn't keep my jobs. Again, I didn't fit in. I felt there was something about life I didn't understand. I tried to be a good colleague but always failed. Was I too sensitive or what? I am sure that it wasn't my job performance that was the problem. I just became more and more depressed. I would smile on the outside while tears were falling on the inside. I couldn't figure out what to do, and I had no one to ask. I was alone and awkward, just as I was as a child within my family. I believed that I was *less than* everybody else and *stupid*. *I must be stupid not to be able to figure out what everybody else seems to know. Why am I always losing?* There were days when suicidal thoughts start creeping in.

As a child and as an adult, I had the same dilemma. Where can I go to ask my questions without being laughed at or bullied? I was so used to being laughed at and ridiculed. I was therefore very shy and on high alert for the smallest sign that I was going to be the target. Little did I know that I was sending out worry signals for any bully to pick up on! It's a natural law that whatever you fear—you attract. I only *thought* that I deserved to be so badly treated. I had really learned my lessons as a child. *I am second-class. I have no rights.* You can't demand anything—not even the basics—such as being washed regularly, having your teeth brushed or being told anything to help you navigate through childhood and life. I never knew what to do in new situations, and I tried to second-guess everything. Nothing was taught to me. *How does the radio work? How do I use a public bathroom? How do I behave around people?* I had thousands of questions, and they all remained unanswered.

In my family, it wasn't possible to learn how to be social or how to behave in "normal ways." My parents didn't have friends, and we rarely had any visitors. My mother's two half-siblings and their spouses were the only people we ever saw. My father's family—we hardly knew them. Parties or social events were extremely rare. There were really only two kinds of evenings—the one when both my parents were home and the other when my dad didn't come home for dinner. Where did he go? I did not know. One day a year my parents hired a babysitter and did something together. Every day, my parents would eat dinner and watch television. They did not have hobbies or read a lot; they did not participate in any sports. Once in a while, we would go for a walk as a family. My mother and father played games together, but my mother always lost, and my father would ridicule her. Every day was pretty much the same. I had few memories of family outings, which were so normal in other kids' lives. I had never been inside a cinema until I went with a girlfriend when I was 13-years-old. I had never been inside a restaurant until I went out with my first husband-to-be.

Today, when I sit and listen to my friends from Switzerland or America, I can't help being somewhat jealous. They talk about family outings, college years and vacations. It all sounds so good. I don't dare tell them about my past. It seems like I grew up on a different planet. I have to find a way to be less defensive about my childhood. Growing up poor shouldn't make me a bad person.

I had no idea how to behave, but I learned early to be like a chameleon. I could change color and behavior in a split second. No one could see the turmoil inside me. I think I had perfected the chameleon behavior before I was four-years-old. I always knew what mood my parents were in at any time. I *sensed* what to do—which face to wear. I thought if I did this, my mother wouldn't cry and my dad wouldn't be angry with me. My antennae were very long, and my nervous system was on high alert. Headaches became part of life. Stress and depression always tried to knock me down. Then there were worries, angst and the hope that no one could see what a useless person I was. That's a lot to carry around every day. Nothing is enjoyable, and it feels like being hunted. I had to become a chameleon and to change in an instant to survive. I would do all this while smiling and pretending to have a free conversation. Pretending... it was the very best of times—too much smiling maybe, laughing too loud and overdoing the talking. *Do people see right through me?* These were things I could agonize over for hours at night while in my bed. I didn't sleep anyway. *I might as well spend time yelling at myself.*

THE BEGINNING OF
THE SOUP

N o one should ever get a pass for child abuse. It is not a valid excuse if you were abused your-self, but perhaps it explains a few things.

I was born 13 years after the Second World War ended. Much of Europe was broken and poor. Life in Europe was and still is very different from life here in the U.S. The war had made an obvious im-pression on all the adults around me. They had gone through the war experience and had learned not to take anything for granted. Everyone was trying to make ends meet. *Even if you had a little extra, you saved it. Money wasn't for fun. Don't you ever forget it!*

My mother grew up in a family that offered her very little support. Her mother was afraid of life and was depressed her whole life. According to my mother, her mother never left the house. Whatever my mother had to do outside the home, she had to do alone. My mother was friendless her whole childhood, and I do believe her lifelong depression began in those early years. My grandmother taught my mother that she was second-class and a useless person...just as my mother did to me. My mother was an obese, uneducated woman who lived with her parents well into her late twenties, which was a bit unusual in those days.

When I take a look at my family through generations, it looks like an endless stream of depressed relatives and sad lives.

I once asked my mother how it felt to lose her mother. As a child, I couldn't imagine such an event. She looked at me with sadness in her eyes and said, "It was such a relief. I didn't have to worry about her anymore...or carry her emotions for her anymore." Amazingly, I had the same feelings when my mother died—sadness and relief at the same time. I do not believe that this is a *rare* case of generational social inheritance. I think it's quite common. We learn from our parents whether we want to or not.

My father had an even stranger childhood than my mother. He didn't talk about his childhood very often. He hardly spoke to his children at all. I believe he was a scared man who hid behind his anger with sarcasm. He would always ridicule my mother and his children when we were afraid. I think it was a way he kept his own fear at bay. He grew up in a very small, old house in the country. He had three brothers and a very sick mother. It has always been kept a whispering secret as to exactly what was wrong with her. I only know that she died young. My grandfather was a cruel man who frequently hit his boys, sometimes so much that my father would run away and hide in the forest for a couple of days. Shortly after the death of my grandmother, my grandfather remarried. The stepmother had two boys of her own and didn't like her stepchildren. I have never understood this. She threw the stepsons out in the street, and they had to fend for themselves. The oldest was 13-years-old and went into an apprenticeship to become a thatcher like his father before him. The youngest was only five-years-old and went to live with a poor shoemaker who had many children of his own. (This uncle committed suicide later in life.) My father was about eleven-years-old and didn't know what to do or where to go. He walked from farm to farm and worked for food. I am sure that the farmhands didn't always treat him with kindness. *Does this explain my father's cruelty?*

I am certain that my father could only survive by setting very rigid and strict rules for himself. He created a life in his own brain that he could live in so that the outer world wouldn't be so threatening. He had to figure out life by himself. He never learned how to be patient and understanding...not with himself or anyone else. There was no room for gray zones or thinking out-of-the-box. My father was always right and no matter how much proof you had to the contrary he wouldn't or couldn't see it. This frozen thinking had a direct effect on the entire family. He lived that way until the day he died.

During the Second World War, my mother's parents opened a small eatery and motel near the beach north of Copenhagen. A lot of regulars had their meals there every day, especially single men, soldiers and widowers. My father, who worked as a mason's hand in those days, began to have his meals at the small eatery. My parents met—two people, each with their sad family story. My grandparents didn't like their relationship and sent my mother away to work in a kitchen at an army base. Unfortunately, my mother had already become pregnant and outside of marriage. In 1957, becoming pregnant outside of marriage was a shameful thing. My mother had two older half siblings who were also born out of wedlock. So, like my grandmother, my mother had shamed herself and the family. In those days, there was only one thing to do...hurry up and get married before the pregnancy began to show too much.

They were married and now had no place to live. It was almost impossible to find inexpensive apartments in those days. I don't know for sure, but I have always had the feeling that my father's employer felt sorry for my parents and helped them out by offering a small living space on the top floor of their villa. I am sure that it was just a room. I can't imagine that it had any kitchen facilities. They had a roof over their head, and that was important. My mother soon became the cleaning lady for the owner's wife, Mrs. Mason. My brother and I were both born there—literally. Most Danish kids were born at home—nothing unusual there. I came into this world on Christmas Day, 1958—364 days after my brother. This didn't give my mother a lot of time between babies. After my arrival, my parents had to move. They found a tiny apartment under the eaves in poor public housing. I grew up in the richest area of Denmark. Few people lived poor like us. There was limited availability of apartments for low-income earners. The difference between my family and the families living around us became more and more apparent as I grew up. I was around six-months old, and my parents finally had an apartment of their own.

My mother continued to clean the villa for many more years. She would go there with children in tow—she couldn't afford a sitter. While my mother was cleaning, we were left in the driveway to look after ourselves. My brother and I, only toddlers, waited forever for her to finish her work. We always had to behave and were told not to make too much noise. After my sister was born, my brother and I tried hard to babysit her while my mother cleaned. She was born only 15 months after me, and I had no idea how to be a "grown-up," as was expected of me. When winter became too harsh, Mrs. Mason would let us "play but not-too-wildly" in the basement party room. In my mind's eye, I can still see the line of chairs up against the wall. I don't remember much about Mrs. Mason except that I didn't like her. She took my mother away from me, left us all alone outside or downstairs and never allowed us to run around and just be kids. I couldn't understand the reason for the whole arrangement. Whether I liked her or not, she always fed us lunch. She made Danish open-faced sandwiches—as many as we liked—but we had to eat outside rain or shine. Today I think of her as a tough lady with a heart.

We lived in our new home until I was four-years-old. I can remember a surprising amount of *stuff* from that early time in my life. The apartment was very small, with only one bedroom. It had no real kitchen, but there was a small, one-burner, gas cooker. We had no bathroom—just a toilet that we shared with the neighbors. Washing clothes and personal hygiene were all done in the small kitchen sink. I do remember a big black pot. My mother would use it to heat the water for washing cloth diapers and clothes. During the short summers in Denmark, she could hang the clothes outside; in the winter, the little apartment became cramped with hanging clothes, and everything smelled wet. My mother was working her butt off and my father, who blamed her for becoming pregnant, didn't help her one bit. I remember the sadness in her eyes already in those early years. I somehow felt responsible for her. What can you do when you are only a toddler? I had a lot of magical thinking. Someone would give us a big house, we would find money, or I could grow up really fast and earn a lot of money. I helped as much as I could and always tried to make my mother happy. My dad had already become the villain in my eyes. I worried a lot to see my mother so sad. The whole world became sad. I didn't know if she could have changed things for the better...had she dared. The atmosphere was just heavy with stuff that a little girl doesn't understand. I remember the somber feeling; happiness was not to be found in that little apartment.

There were no stores nearby, and my mother had to walk about two miles to get to a small supermarket and with two—and soon three—small children. It was a long, cold walk. I do not think my dad helped her carry food home once in his entire life. She returned home to a cold apartment with crying, needy children. She had nowhere to get help or understanding. She became just as needy as her children. In this dysfunctional family circle, no one was thriving. My brother and I were pretty much left alone—fed a little and diapers changed a bit. Left alone.

My sister was born 15 months after my birth. At that point, the apartment became way too small for all of us. Outside the apartment, next to our front door, was a small room that my parents rented for a small sum. That's where my brother and I spent a lot of our time alone. I can't remember if we were together in one bed or if we each had a bed. I do remember the loneliness, the fear and the crying out loud. My mother conveniently believed that crying in children was good for the development of lungs. So, my brother and I cried for hours and finally gave up in the end and went to sleep. I can't remember if there was a window in this little storage room. *Was it dark in there? Did we have any toys? Could strangers come and go?* All I know is that when I think of that little room, my stomach knots up. It is fear—total fear.

I have to stop all these questions before I scare myself again all these years later.

Many years later when we were adults, I had a conversation with my brother about our solitary confinement cell. When I began to describe what I remembered, he became totally pale and could not listen. He disassociated, and even though he sat next to me, he was no longer *with me.* I told my brother that we were like the Children of Romania. When Nicolae Ceausescu and his wife were dethroned in 1989, the world was finally able to see how they had ruined their country. He wanted his people to have many children and populate his country. It didn't matter to him that most people were dirt poor and had no way of taking care of their offspring. He had a solution. Many inadequate homes for orphans were built all over the country, but no one was trained to look after the children. Hundreds of thousands of babies and young children were lying in bed without even minimal human contact. They had a little food but not much more. Many articles were written about the physical and emotional scars that were inflicted upon these children. Whether or not there was any physical abuse, it became clear that these children could not develop without proper human contact such as hugs and affection. I feel my brother, and I lived a bit like that in our first years. Of course, we were taken care of better than those sad Romanian children, but I still feel that I can relate to them.

I am alone. I am crying, and no one hears. There was no contact from the outside world…no physical contact. I think my mother world turn over in her grave if she knew how I felt about those early years. Did she wake up every morning with the purpose to hurt my brother and me?

The answer is no. My mother was so overwhelmed and alone that the neglect happened. Did she ever stop to think that *she* was just dishing it out and lashing out? Did she ever reflect upon what would become of her children later in their lives? I have no answer to these questions. All I do know is that it was sad being alone in that little room. It was equally sad being inside the apartment with all the unsolved problems and unresolved emotions. This was the stuff that I was picking up without even knowing it.

My father didn't care about my mother or his children for that matter. He once proclaimed with pride, "I never even touched or picked you up until you were more than a year."

I can't remember him during those early years. My mother was scared of everything, including my father. She probably cried as much as her children. It became clear to me at a very young age that it was my duty to make my mother happy and to meet her needs…a world upside down. This was a burden that had me stooped over like an old woman before I was a teenager. I always felt that I was wrong or doing something wrong since my mother was so tired and so unhappy. I was just a little girl and couldn't see the bigger picture.

My mother's tears had taught me before I was four, how to BE. The early misunderstanding of my role in the world—*The Soup* as I call it—began so early that I can't remember life without the guilt, stupidity, and feeling "less than others." I felt sorry for being needy, and I tried not to ask for anything. I felt sorry for my mother that my dad didn't help her with anything, and I felt that there was something I was supposed to do...but I could never figure out what it was. I knew I had to do something; my very life depended on it.

My brother and I were hardly ever supervised. We were sent outside to play at a very young age— just toddlers in an unsafe environment. My brother often talked about the time I almost drowned in a lake that was right next to the apartment building. I don't remember any of it, but it has haunted him. He was one-year older and may have felt responsible.

Sometimes I think my parents believed that we were born adults. Today the social services would have taken us away from them. We lived a little outside of town, and there was some traffic on the little road to the apartment building. The small children from the other apartments were also outside without parents and accidents did happen. I remember a four-year-old girl being hit by a car. She ran right in front of it—sort of a game we played. Let's see who dares to run close to the cars. We had no concept of consequence. We children were tough with each other.

It appears to me that all the families were in chaos, but I can only see that in the rear-view mirror.

Once as an adult, I went to visit—to see if I correctly remembered everything. It looked beautiful with the little lake full of ducks, and the apartment building had been modernized. I froze and couldn't go up the staircase.

As I mentioned, my little sister was born 15 months after me. *My parents obviously didn't think this through.* I believe that the sister rivalry and sister envy began very early. My new baby sister was living in the apartment with mom and dad. I was crying in the storage room off the public hallway.

It didn't help that my parents believed that my sister's needs were more important. The crying and the resentment were always present. We had no room, no proper kitchen, and no laundry area. So now, the chaos and the dysfunction were complete. *How can we live in this tiny apartment? The grocery-shopping trip with three small children was horrible, especially in the winter.* My mother was often very impatient with us. She had no time in her busy day. I always felt as though I was in the way. I do not ever remember a time when she sang or read to us. I began to feel that invisibility was the best bet. Don't be a burden.

CRAZY CHILDHOOD

W hen I was about four-years-old, we moved to another public housing project. There weren't many to choose from as they were tucked away as an embarrassment to the rich area just north of Copenhagen. The move wasn't too many miles away and was done in one day. My mother seemed a little happier for a while. We now had about 600 square feet and an old-fashioned, tenant-shared washing machine in the basement.

This new apartment was a big upgrade, and my mother was happy to see that there was a small convenience store nearby. For bigger shopping, we had to take a bus. I hated those shopping trips mostly because my mother was totally stressed out. Everything was too expensive for her, and we all wanted to see and touch everything. We ran around the store.

We were wild kids. My mother lost control of everything. The other shoppers gave my mother the evil eye. When the shopping was finally done, we had to carry it all home, and it was heavy. My mother was physically strong as a horse, but emotionally, she was worn out. The weekly shopping trip took her over the edge, and she would come down with one of her asthma attacks at the moment we reached the staircase to our apartment. She had carried the heavy load with no strain, but suddenly she couldn't cope anymore. It was pretty much the same shopping scenario every week. I felt so sorry for her that I began to hate the shopping trips too. My dad would have driven right passed us on his motor bike without helping, of that I am certain.

The small apartment on the second floor had four rooms—a small toilet with a little sink and an adequate kitchen. There was no hot water. The only form of heat came from an old wood and coal stove in the corner of the living room. The biggest room was the living room, and the next biggest was the dining room. There were two small bedrooms.

When I first saw our new kitchen, I noticed a strange-looking thing hanging high up on the wall. As a little girl, I didn't know what it was, but it had my interest…numbers, buttons and a little handle. It was a special gas meter that ensured that the tenant couldn't use any gas unless it was paid for in advance.

It had a slot for coins but took only one specific kind of coin, and it would only allow for a limited amount at a time. Unless the meter was fed this coin, the gas would stop in the middle of the cooking and baking. My mother was always on the lookout for the right kind of coin. She constantly checked to see if the gas was still on. The whole thing was annoying, but the worst part was that this stupid machine was hung so high on the wall that it couldn't be reached without climbing onto the counter. My mother either climbed up there herself or lifted one of the children up there to put coins in the meter. There was no end to the inconvenience of being poor. The tenants couldn't be trusted with a gas bill at the end of the month like "normal" people were trusted.

Many years later, we were finally given the green light for normal billing, and the gas inspector didn't have to come once a month to collect the coins from the meter. My mother was happy about that, but the meter didn't get disconnected for many more years. She still had to get up to the meter and feed it, but she could reuse the same coins again and again. It was convenient to the gas company and no one else.

When we first lived there, all of the children slept in one bedroom. We had so much more room than before. We were so happy that we didn't have to go outside in the public hallway to go to the toilet. I had never seen such a big apartment before in my life. I remember running around looking at it all. There were two buildings with six apartments in each, and in-between them was a big parking lot. It was used more like a playground as most tenants couldn't afford a car. A small grass field with a sandbox sat behind the parking lot.

I would often come in from playing, eat my dinner and then go straight to bed without being washed. This could continue for several days in a row. My hair was stiff with sand from playing in the sandbox. My bed sheets became a bit itchy after a while. It was a huge deal to get the laundry done in our family; therefore, the bed linens weren't changed very often. Personal hygiene wasn't much easier. When we were really small, I do remember sharing an old-fashioned sink tub with my brother. The real problem began when we couldn't fit in there anymore. My mother would heat a big, heavy pot of water. Then she would carry it from the kitchen, through the dining room and small hallway and then into the little toilet room in the back of the apartment. There we had a tiny, little sink. The room wasn't heated. I remember standing on an ice-cold stone floor while my mother washed me. My lips would quiver with cold, and I kept asking her to pour some hot water over me. There was never enough hot water in the pot to keep me warm. She would dry me with a thin towel until I stopped shaking. Then she had to start all over again for my sister and brothers. *Who was looking after the other kids while she was in the bathroom with one of us?* My father was nowhere to be found—nothing new about that. No wonder we didn't get washed every day. I loved the feeling of a clean bed and a clean body more than anything...preferably on the same day. Living poor wasn't easy.

When I was about seven-years-old, the apartment building got central heating, which meant radiators in every room, except the toilet room. There wasn't room for one, but a shower was installed in the tiny room. The whole place was soaking wet after every shower. I loved the feeling of warm water running over me. The showers had to be very short as hot water was expensive. My father was a very stingy man. Bathing was not an everyday affair. I remember mold forming on the lower walls of this little room. In the winter, it was damp, and our towels could not get dry. It always smelled damp and a bit moldy. I never thought anything of it as a child. It was just part of life.

Unfortunately, the actual heater was installed in the laundry room downstairs. We had to say good-bye to the old-fashioned laundry machine. We didn't have room or money for a washing machine, so we had to take a bus to the laundromat. All the wealthy people around us had washers and dryers, and there was only one laundromat in the area, which was many miles away. I remember my embarrassment—standing up during the bus ride with several enormous sacks of smelly laundry, filled with bedding and clothing for six people. My father did have a motorbike with a sidecar. He had it most of his life but never once offered to drive the clothes there and back. The motorbike was for his pleasure and used in the summer when he did do some work.

Each apartment had a small vegetable garden. My mother would grow strawberries, potatoes, rhubarbs and a few other vegetables. The growing season in Denmark is very short but, for a couple of months, we had the best potatoes and strawberries in the world. I loved going to the little garden, picking the berries and digging up the new potatoes. The huge rhubarb leaves would be the carrying baskets. I can still see myself standing in the rain, with a rhubarb leaf as an umbrella, while eating the sour, bitter stalk. I loved the smell of the earth but hated that my mother had to work so hard. Her feelings were with me all the time. I took her feelings and hardships unto me and carried them as if they were mine. This took a lot of my energy away from me.

I remember running downstairs to see everything outside. As I ran out the front door, I met the children of the neighborhood, and they scared me. There were many kids there, and they all stared at this little newcomer. First, I hated their curious eyes and, for a moment, I wished we had never moved. Over the next weeks, months and years, the relationships that I had with these children became the most stable part of my life. We all lived in problem families. Dysfunction was normal, and we didn't know any better. There were children of all ages, and we all had the same wish—to stay outside as much as possible. We played all kinds of games, and many of them were not particularly safe. None of the children had any adult supervision. So, we learned the hard way. The older children were hitting the smaller children, but they also protected them from strangers and other dangers.

We were a strange mass of children living in a form of anarchy, but as a group, we had a ton of fun. There was a boy named Sven. He was our *leader*. He was quite tall and very strong boy. Sven, who was one-year-older than I was, ruled with toughness, but he was also fair as only kids can be. He came from a family of severe alcoholics. His older brother was often seen vomiting, yelling and screaming—drunk out of his skull. The first time it happened, he was no more than a teenager. The children didn't want him in the pack. He acted more like the grownups and was totally out of control. Once, when I was about 12, one of the dads came walking by us children and all of a sudden, he lifted up my skirt and began to fondle me—right there in front of everybody. Sven got up and hit him really hard and told him never to come near any of the girls again. It felt safe to be Sven's good friend, and I looked up to him during all my childhood. *It was as if we knew better than the adults exactly what was right or wrong. We did so much crazy stuff. It is surprising we survived it all.*

We were all very spontaneous and loved to play. There were no boundaries put upon us from our parents. My mother often stood at the window. She said she worried a lot, but I do not remember her ever leaving the apartment to go down stairs to teach us something or tell us what we could or couldn't do. Oh, wait. She mentioned that we were not allowed to play in the blacksmith's backyard. His yard, which backed up to "our land," was filled with old cars, backhoes and lots of other dangerous equipment. So, where did we go? Yes, it was a lot of fun as we pretended driving the old cars. We made up a fun game too—let see who can run around the longest and fastest without ever touching the ground, jumping from car to scrap metal, and then onto another car and so on.

We did get hurt a bit but never enough to make us stop going there. My sister did have a bad fall one day and was bleeding from her forehead. Sven carried her home. My mother went into her usual panic attack, but we would still go to the blacksmith and play. When I was about nine-years-old, a young boy

and I found an unopened beer inside an old trac-
tor, and we wanted to drink it. We managed to open
it with some old piece of metal, and we drank the
whole thing. We both got a little funny—another
little secret I kept from my mother.

My mother never actually went to see where we
were and sometimes we were miles away. I think she
was very happy to have the apartment to herself—
out of sight out of mind. I can't know for sure, but I
always had the feeling that my mother would overeat
when she was home alone. I do remember her buying cookies and sweets, but they were never served. I
often wondered where the goodies went. I certainly
didn't get them. Why was it only the adults who were
allowed to eat all the sweets they wanted? There was
never any understanding of adult behavior.

My mother didn't only eat sweets. She would
pretty much eat anything to soothe her nerves. It
was mostly done in hiding, but my father must have
known. From time to time, he would humiliate her
for her lack of self-control. I am sure that didn't
help at all. I wish that eating disorders were known
and discussed back then. It might have helped her.
Instead, it was yet another problem to hide and keep
to herself. From time to time, my mother would try
to lose weight. It wasn't easy, as she firmly believed
that weight loss was equal to being sick. In fact, she
was a real hypochondriac; her fear of cancer was

greater than her sadness about being too big. Diets were doomed from the start.

My mother also feared the ocean, and she insisted that we learned to swim very early. We lived about three miles from the beach, and my mother sent my little sister and me for swimming lessons. The two of us would bike to the beach, take the lessons, and bike back. I believe I was six years and my sister a bit younger. The lessons began in early June, and the water was freezing cold. But the swimming instructor would push us from the pier if we didn't get in fast enough. We both loved to swim, and my sister was better at it than I was; I hated that. My sister and I would go to the beach all the time. My mother would make a lunch box for us, and we would spend the whole day there. Sometimes the waves were pretty high, but we swam anyway. Can you imagine that happening today; two young kids at the beach alone? But we had a great time. One day when I was a teenager, a couple of boys decided to throw me into the water from the pier. One kid was holding my arms, the other my leg, and they were swinging me back and forth. After counting to three, one kid let my legs go, but the other didn't let go of my arms. I fell hard into the pier, scraped my left side pretty bad and fell into the water. The air was beaten out of me, and I couldn't swim. Fortunately, the boys jumped in and helped me out. I was so hurt I couldn't bike home; I walked with my bike for what seems to be an eternity. I was more worried about my mother's reaction than my pain.

Back to the kids. There was one kid who was a little strange. He didn't fit into the pack. I remember sitting and playing in the sand. I think I was around seven or eight. He was standing behind me. All of a sudden, he opened his trousers and began to pee on me. I didn't know what to do. I moved a little, but he moved with me. The smell was awful, and the thought that somebody was peeing on me was beyond unpleasant. This incident represents the dysfunction and the "warped-normal" during my childhood. I ran home crying. Fortunately, it was after we had a shower installed.

Once when I was about 11-years-old, a friend and I decided to go for a long walk. We had no water with us. We just began walking. After a while, I said, "Let's go visit my aunt." She lived a good ten miles away. When we got there, she wasn't home. We just turned around and walked back. We were gone for many hours, but I do not think that anyone missed us. It was in the days before cell phones, and I doubt that we would have called anyway. My friend and I had hoped that my Aunt Anna and her husband would be there to drive us home. Money—we didn't have. We couldn't take a bus, but we had learned early to become self-reliant—altogether not a bad thing. I was never given any pocket money. I knew other kids did have some spending money, but I would never have dared ask.

We climbed trees in the spring and summer. We sat in the wild cherry trees, eating the fruit until we all had stomach aches. We built small houses out of old wood, which we found on building sites. We would hammer and saw the wood. I swear some of the children were not much more than toddlers when we did this. These little ones were being looked after by their older siblings and were just part of the pack. One house was so big that ten or more children could fit in there. In the parking lot, we played badminton, hide-and-seek and many other fun games.

I remember a game we played with pocket knives. We would throw knives at each other in a certain pattern. Amazingly, we didn't get hurt too often. We learned to be fast and to have quick reactions.

In the winter, the kids would build igloos and go skating. There was a small lake not too far away. We would put on our skates and walk with them on over the farmer's field and to the frozen lake. We would hammer a hole in the ice. When the oldest among us declared the ice thick enough, we would start skating. There was never an adult involved in this decision-making process.

Only once in my childhood did I see someone fall through the ice and into the lake. Wet socks, however, were not a big deal…happened all the time. We were poor, and skates were expensive—so we got old used ones. One year I didn't have the right size skates. They were way too small. I loved to be with the kids and didn't want to sit out. So, I went skating without any socks. Every time I came home my feet were blue and numb, and when they began to defrost, they hurt like mad. It didn't deter me one bit. Tough kids like us had a good tolerance for pain.

The gang of kids had a small hill on "our land." One winter it was bitter cold, but we didn't have any snow. We all missed the snow but decided to throw big buckets of water onto the slope and make an "ice ride." We would stand on a big piece of plastic and let it slide down the icy slope. It was a fun ride, but we were all pretty badly bruised. Some kids did fall hard and got concussions; they didn't come back for a few days. *I am sure they didn't see a doctor. I am convinced they never told their parents what they were doing.* It was like two parallel worlds—we had our world, and the parents had their world. We didn't mingle a lot.

I certainly never told my worrying mother about my freezing feet, swollen ankles, bruised ribs and other sores from falling down from tree branches. I do remember that I once got a rusty nail right through my fingernail and through my finger. It really hurt, and when I pulled the nail out, it began to bleed quite a bit. My first thought was that mother would go nuts if she saw this and she would have a panic attack. I walked home and went into the bathroom where my parents kept a small first-aid kit. I once heard that pure alcohol was a germ-killer and very good on open sores. I poured some over my injured finger. I almost fainted. The pain was so strong that I had to bite my lips not to scream out loud. The alcohol helped the bleeding, and it was easy to put on a little bandage. At dinner, my mother asked why I was wearing a bandage, and I said that it was a little nothing. My nail still grows out funny. Tetanus? I had never heard of that.

It is amazing how we learned to take care of ourselves on a physical level. I learned what my body could do, and I trusted my reflexes and my strength. I became a very good athlete...not that I ever did anything about it. Sports were expensive and looked down upon in my family.

We children never talked about our families and the emotional problems we had. I do not think we had words for it all; it was sort of normal to us. As we watched what the adults did and didn't do, our boundaries for what was acceptable were pushed far over the normal range. We children were always very loyal to each other, and we never laughed and ridiculed other children for what their parents did. Seeing a parent totally drunk peeing in the bushes or falling all over the place was very common and seeing another dad sleeping with someone else's wife at dusk, or knowing that a pedophile lived amongst us was just a fact. And we didn't know it wasn't normal for these things to happen right in front of our eyes; it was part of our little world within the public housing project. It was a known to us all that he molested his own children, even went to prison for a while. But as soon as he was out, he went back and did it again. His poor daughter was never part of the pack—never part of anything. She was her dad's slave and could never leave his side. One winter, when all the kids were out playing, she stood next to her dad and watched. Her hands were freezing, and she said she would run upstairs and get some gloves. Her dad flatly told her she wasn't allowed to go anywhere and there was nothing she could do. He and only he had rights over her. I was very young but felt like hitting the bastard. (He later became my mother's good friend. What a horrifying thought.)

The children in this housing complex knew that the adults were dysfunctional and not to be trusted. When people today talk about how other people misbehave, it's hard for me to react correctly; it takes a lot to shock me. Often, I think people get upset over nothing—*sissies*. I know I have seen way too much and at a very young age.

SNIPPET FIVE:

SAD TEEN

I loved this group of kids but the teenage years set in and I began to be more aware of myself. I slowly grew away from playing and began to prepare for adulthood, whatever that means. There were no real friends in school and being really shy about my changing body, I isolated myself more and more. There were no longer any fun outlets and no fellowship. My emotional problems began to show their ugly faces. The teenage years are never easy, and I began to hate my family, my life and myself in general. It was during those years that *My Soup* really began to ruin my life, and I often thought of ending it all.

I had one very good friend named Jesper. He was a boy from school. His parents were never home, and we spent a ton of time together. We walked his dog, worked on homework, played together and listened to music. His family was so accustomed to me being around that, when his parents came home and made dinner, they just put an extra plate on the table. I slowly became part of his family. With them, I had fun! I wouldn't have been able to cope if not for my friend Jesper. Unfortunately, he met a girl he liked, and she didn't want me around. Not only did I lose a friend, but I also lost my safe haven and my new family. I became lonely.

It was around the time that I lost Jesper to his new friend that my first suicidal thoughts emerged—ever so slowly—from my brain. These thoughts didn't come to me as a complete thought like *I am going to kill myself.* They formed…oh so slowly. I felt invisible and left out of the world. I hated that feeling and yet I didn't want to be seen or discovered, as I believed I would receive harsh judgment. I was very different from the other teenagers—at least I thought so. Everywhere I turned, I could only see a dead end. *Do I really want to die?* I probably didn't want to die, but I certainly didn't want to live with all the sadness either.

I felt awkward and imagined unsolvable problems in everything. I had no one to talk to and nowhere to turn. I was feeling lonely and thought that all the other teens knew it all. I tried to smile and pretend I was happy, more than likely overdoing the old, familiar act. It's easy to go overboard. I didn't know about moderation and never felt real, honest-to-goodness happiness.

I remember one day sitting in the school classroom. A boy who I secretly liked a lot said to me, "You are always to irritatingly happy, it's annoying." My little world with its theater fell apart. I became so stressed that I actually fainted. I really wanted to disappear in shame, and my body did it for me. My mantra was in full bloom! *Why don't I ever know how to be anything but a stupid idiot?*

Things can quickly get out of hand for a teenager, and I was as ripe as could be. I never acted on my thoughts, but I had suicidal thoughts off and on for many years, even into adulthood.

Whenever I hear of a child or teenager who has committed suicide, I wonder how their years were before that sad act. Bullying, bad home life or a combination of the two; whatever it might have been, there must have been signs. Sadness and depression in children are different from depression in adults. At least that is my experience. As a child, you have no choice, nowhere to go and parents, peers, and school keeps piling on stuff. You can't say no and opt out, and can't seek help without permission. And you have no way of knowing that what you feel is not normal. If you have a bad day, no one takes you seriously because whatever bugs you is only "kid stuff."

Certainly, adults around me didn't think children could have real problems. *Get over it and don't bother me.* I wish somebody would have seen my sadness and taken me seriously the few times I tried to tell. Children try their hardest to fit in, and they are very resilient, so I guess it can be hard to see the signs, but I cry when I see sad children. It is so easy to blame the child for bad behavior, but I do firmly believe that all children are born with a will to please and to be good children. It's only when adults don't let them be good that things go wrong. It is sometimes wrong expectations that make a child take a bad turn. My parents expected me to be in a certain way, and whether I wanted it or not, it happened. So, if we could believe that all children are good and clever, and then treat them accordingly, wouldn't they just become that...good? *Am I oversimplifying things?*

When I am out and about, and I hear and see parents treat their children with disrespect, I wonder where these children will be in ten to 15 years. The parents don't listen to their kids. They yell at them or call them names. Parents demand respect from their children, but I believe respect is something we should earn. A couple of years ago, I was in a supermarket and saw two women talking. One of them had a small, three-year-old child in a stroller. The women talked for a long time, and the child got a little impatient and began to talk to his mother.

At first, the child spoke quietly, but then he became louder and louder. The mother ignored him for a long time. Finally, the parent turned to the child and yelled, right into his face, "Shut up! You are the worst child in the whole world." Then she turned right back to her conversation. The friend didn't react. I didn't know what to do. I smiled as lovingly as I could to the little boy but his eyes were filled with sadness, and I couldn't hold his gaze. His humiliation was written all over his face. This stranger (me) now knew that he was the worst child in the whole world. I wanted to go over and hug him and yell at his mother, but I was afraid of doing so. I regretted my lack of action many times since this incident. Standing up for that little boy might have been worth a black eye.

Maybe I am too sensitive. When I see situations like that one, my heart cries along with my own inner children. *You are no better than all the adults who didn't see you when you needed them.*

SNIPPET SIX:
DREADED SCHOOL YEARS

I grew older and began to see the dysfunction around me. I would ask my mother question like, "Why can't we live somewhere else?" She always said that she loved being exactly where she was. I think she felt that she was a little bit better than the other people living there. "We are not as bad." In a way, her very low self-esteem wasn't threatened. The children in the neighborhood pretty much raised each other and themselves. It was an unsafe and stressful way to grow up. We all coped as children do, but we didn't learn the difference between unsafe and safe behaviors. In a sense, we were wild.

I have always hated questions such as, "What would you like to do when you get older?" I had no ideas about anything—no ambitions, no choices and no needs or wants. These were drained out of me before I started first grade. The mention of school sent chills down my spine. The more dysfunction at home, the more problems with school and peers. I don't know why I even use the word peers. I never really fitted in. I had a girlfriend from time-to-time, but I was one of those girls who would hang on to every newcomer in the hope that this time I would make a real friend.

And here it was again—that *something* I couldn't figure out. One thing was obvious. I grew up in a very rich part of Denmark, and I stood out like a sore thumb. I was often unwashed. I wore the same clothes for many days and didn't own a toothbrush until the school dentist totally humiliated me. I couldn't afford to buy the things that the other children could. I always wondered how the girls smelled so good. They had parents that drove cars, and they had teeth too! These parents seemed to care for their children. I thought there was something wrong with me. I tried to fit in. I had honestly never heard of such things as body lotion, face creams and makeup.

The first school years weren't so bad, and I wasn't particularly aware of what was going on. I really liked learning to read and write, and I loved math. The problem began when the other children found me to be an easy target for teasing. They noticed that I was different and, as time went on, it became a serious problem. In my early teenage years, the bullying was constant and often got physical. I never complained to anyone. *No one would listen anyway.*

School became more and more stressful for me. Instead of paying attention to the teachings, I used more and more of my time worrying about recess. I tried to be tough. I never cried, at least not on the outside. I was very good at crying silently, with my tears running on the inside. I became scared of everything—just being in school and going to and from school. Questions from the teachers and the school dentist scared me too. (In Denmark, most public schools have dentists.) The first time I went to see him, I had so many bad teeth that he screamed at me. Without giving any anesthesia, he filled the many cavities. It was as if he was trying to teach me a lesson about oral hygiene through the pain. It never entered his brain that I, a six-year-old, was not the one to be blamed. I had never owned a toothbrush. Every year when I was called to see the dentist, I was so scared I almost went into shock.

As school went on, I also stopped raising my hand in class and became a false, smiling idiot who hoped that no one would notice my sadness and shame. I began to take long walks in total solitude. I loved the forests and the fields. I was never scared when walking alone in the fields. It was people who scared me. My mother found it troubling, and she thought I was antisocial. Can't you just stay home for once? Can't you be like other children? Why are you always so tired? It didn't matter what I did or didn't do, I never could get it right. Looking back at it all, I think that either I was a really good actor or my teachers just didn't care. Why didn't anybody see this sad little girl?

The boys could physically hurt you, but the girls were emotionally destructive. When I was in seventh or eighth grade, we had to go on a weeklong field trip. I was excited about going to the mainland of Denmark, which I, of course, knew about but had never visited. I was looking forward to a long train and a ferry ride too. I dreaded packing my few belongings, which the others girls would go through and laugh about them. The public-school system was paying for the trip, and there was no way out. I braced myself and tried to get mentally tough. When we arrived at the hostel, we were sent to our rooms to unpack and figure out who was going to sleep where and with whom. Boys were on one side of the hallway and girls were on the other with three or four children to every room. No one wanted to be in a room with me...not even the girl I thought was a friend at that moment in time. I had learned early not to be a tattletale, as I knew it would backfire on me. The teachers would not let me sleep alone and blamed me for being difficult and obstinate.

The teacher assigned me to a bedroom with three other girls. There were two bunk beds in each room, and I was in the lower bed. After dinner, the dreaded moment of going to our bedrooms could no longer be postponed. I didn't want to be a problem and pretended to be asleep right away. Shortly after the light went out, the girls began to badmouth me in the nastiest way possible. I am sure they knew I was awake and knew that they were hurting me bad. *Teenage girls can be really awful when they are together in a pack*. One problem was that one of the girls had to share a bunk bed with me—actually touching the same bed as me. *How nasty.*

After a while, they forced me to sleep on the floor, and the bitching didn't stop there. It felt like it lasted for hours and hours. I had never been so hurt in my entire life. They just downright hated me, and everything about me. They hated how I looked and behaved—nothing was off the table.

At one point, I had had enough. I got up, grabbed my covers and left the room. I was hoping one of the extra bedrooms was unlocked and that I could use one of the beds in there. Otherwise, I would sleep outside on the grass—anything to get away from these girls and their evil tongues. I cried a lot that night and feared the coming of morning. I was afraid of the teachers for taking a room for myself, but I was more scared of the girls. (I don't think that I need to go into more details of that field trip, but it was a very long and sad week.) One girl did come to me and apologized, but I never trusted any of them again. My hope was to one day have a friend I could talk about my family problems. This hope was firmly dashed. I was not going to trust anybody with anything ever again.

At recess, I was always worried. I never knew what would come in my direction. When I was 13-years-old, many of my peers had tried to smoke, and it became a burden to say "no" a hundred thousand times. One day I took the cigarette and smoked. It was horrible, and I hoped that I never had to do it again. It felt good to be part of *something*, even if it was just with the bad kids who smoked. I certainly didn't have the money for it, and I began to steal some of my Dad's cigarettes. I didn't like any of it, and the smoking made me feel bad. I continued and didn't stop again until I was 31-years-old and almost died from a blood clot in my lung.

I have never been giving any pocket money or any money at all, and it was difficult to be a young teenager and never have any money. I found myself a little job, cleaning at a bakery shop every afternoon. They didn't pay very much, but it was nice to have my own money. What a shame that so much of it went towards cigarettes. As my teenage years continued, so did my need for money. I began to babysit a lot. My big dream was to be dressed like the other girls, but that was out of my reach. Sometimes my parents would buy nice clothes or shoes for my sister, and they would tell me that they couldn't afford to buy for both of us. "You are a big girl, and you can understand this." I certainly didn't want to add to the already enormous feeling of stupidity that I carried around every day. I couldn't afford to feel the feelings that came with my parent's denial of my needs. I hardened myself. *Who needs new clothes anyway? I am beyond that.* In reality, I hated seeing my sister walking around in the kind of clothes I would have loved to have for myself. I felt it was a kind of punishment. *What did I do to be treated in this way?*

Once our teacher decided that we should all go and see a show in Copenhagen. The girls all wanted to wear long skirts or dresses. There was no way in hell I could afford something like that. I pretended that I didn't want to go and that theater was overrated. Inside I cried. I would have loved to go to a theater, and I had hardly ever been to Copenhagen and never at night. My teacher scolded me for being difficult and obstinate. *I hate her.* How stupid could she be? How could she not know that I didn't have the money to buy a long skirt? I couldn't tell her, out of some weird sense of loyalty to my parents. I hated to admit that we were poor; it always set me up for more bullying. My new armor was to fake it. *I don't care what you think or say. Who cares to see theater anyway— overrated stuff?*

When I was about 12-years-old, the burden of carrying all my fears alone was overwhelming. Nightmares and night terrors began to set in. I would be totally paralyzed with fear. I feared nighttime. I feared the darkness. I feared people in the street. I feared my parents. I began to believe that I would have a short life. A pattern began during those years and would last for most of my life. It has become a bit better the last ten years, but I never know when the same night terror will haunt me again. It was every night, sometimes several times a night and to the point where I would try not to go to bed.

Nightmares have many subjects, and they change all the time, and when I wake up, I know it was just a dream. (I will share some of my dreams later in this book.) Night terrors are different from nightmares. For me, the terror is the same every time, and when I wake up, it is incredibly real. I believe it is real every single time.

It's always about a man entering my bedroom. The terror will usually begin at that time when I am just about to fall asleep or have only slept a few minutes. I am not awake but not fast asleep either. The night terror is always happening in the exact room where I am at that moment—in a hotel, my own house or a friend's bedroom. This makes it very real. Every time, I am pale and sweating. I am overcome by a fear so enormous that no logical thoughts enter my brain.

I am like a haunted animal that is too scared to run. I can't do anything but lie there paralyzed, waiting for this horrible person to enter my bedroom. I hear the floorboards. I hear the door open. I hear his breathing. I know that this person is going to hurt me in the most brutal way. First, he will sexually abuse and sadistically torture me and then slowly kill me. It's always the same. His hand comes around the doorframe and, at that moment, I wake up. Terrified. I am 100% sure there is a person in my room. It takes quite a while for my brain to realize that it is "just" a night terror again. I usually take about a good 30 minutes before the stiffness leaves my body and my heartbeat becomes normal again. Finally, I will find myself brave enough to go get some water and check out my surroundings. It takes a long time before I am ready to fall asleep again and often the whole thing restarts. I was worn out for years.

SNIPPET SEVEN:
DYSFUNCTION

I was tired and worn out from too many terrifying nights. My schoolwork and life, in general, suffered as a result. I didn't tell anyone about my night terrors for many years. My dad would have thought it funny and would have purposely scared me even more. He already loved to stand behind a door in the dark to scare the life out of me. My mother would have been so scared for herself that she wouldn't have talked about anything else. She would have treated my "secret" in a disrespectful way and belittled it. In the end, the thought that her daughter was weird would have overwhelmed her so much that I would have had to help her deal with it. As usual, I was the mother of my mother, and her needs were to be met and not mine. She was insensitive to problems that didn't directly involve her.

I still remember the first time I dared to share my story. I think I was about 27 years old or so. I was with a new girlfriend who seemed to be a caring person. I was very terrified to tell; maybe she would think I was ready for an insane asylum. In the end, my need to finally share this horror was bigger than my fear. I began to explain why I was always tired and, with a small whispering voice, I began to share my secret. As I was describing the details, I became panicky, and my whole body was shaking. I began to cry. I had carried this alone for so many years. When I was done, I had a huge headache and felt like I had just run a marathon. My new friend didn't run away and was very understanding. Thank God. I do not know if I would have been able to take it if she had laughed at me. I had great hopes that telling would make it go away but that didn't happen. It was nice not to carry such a secret alone anymore.

Depression was an ongoing theme in my family. Fear, anger and negative thinking seemed to run in our DNA. When I think of my mother's and grand-mother's depressions, I realize how hard it was to get out of this circle of generational *Soup*. It's as if I was born into and was expected to be like the women in past generations. My mother had no idea about boundaries, and I felt invaded most of my life. In her mind, we were the same. We had the same likes and dislikes, and she could even read my mind. Even my body belonged to her. If she needed affection, she would take it. She didn't see it as an invasion to come into the toilet when I was doing my business. I am not talking about an infant here. She also wanted me in the toilet with her. She would try anything to trick me in there with her. I hated it all—the smells of her. I knew that we both knew it was wrong. It was forbidden to have any other thoughts than her thoughts. I belonged to her, and any rebellion was met with a message of "you are a bad girl." There is no doubt that my mother was depressed but she also had a way to make it my problem. I felt she could cry whenever it was to her advantage and, since everything was my fault, it was my duty to make her happy no matter what she had done. All I could do was to hurry up and be the person she wanted. *You little Kirsten are only as smart as I let you be. You are not to have any needs and wants. Tears and complaints are only for a mother to use.*

I make my mother look like a monster, but she could also be nice and caring. I think that the two sides of her made it very difficult, if not impossible, for me to understand her. I didn't know that a person could be so two-faced. Since she could be very loving when she wanted to be, I thought for sure that I was to blame for her bad side, just as she indicated. When she had a good day or when we children behaved to her liking, she could be very nice. I especially remember sitting at the dining table with my home-work or my coloring book while she ironed. I still love the smell of clothes being ironed. She would sometimes sing with me and comb my hair nicely, not hard and angry as some other days. We would go for a nice walk and talk. I loved those times. She also made Christmas very special and lovely. Even my dad was involved with making Christmas Eve pretty and wonderful. We never had many presents, but it was the only day of the year that I felt really safe. I knew that we wouldn't have any problems. We sang together as a family. We had a real nice meal and, as poor as we were, there were sweets, fruit and nuts. We didn't see much of these during the rest of the year. I loved Christmas and still do.

In Denmark, the whole month of December is festive and cozy. This atmosphere is present wher-ever you go. The streets are dressed with many beautiful lights, and it smells of special Christmas treats. Homes are dressed-to-the-nines with Danish Christmas gnomes and decorations and, of course, Christmas trees. The trees are always real, and the smell of pine is in the air. We always dress the tree with electric lights but, on Christmas Eve, real can-dles adore the tree. Christmas is celebrated on the evening of December 24th.

Denmark is so far north that the days are short and very cold. Everybody tries their best to make this dark time as cozy as possible. Homemade cookies get baked, and homemade decorations are hung. Candles sparkle at every meal and special seasonal drinks and foods are served. Excitement is in the air and expectations are high. Every Christmas must be exactly as fabulous as the last one—or perhaps a little better. Of course, presents are important, but the Christmas spirit is equally as important. The singing, the togetherness and the overall feeling of festivities were more important and bigger than any gifts.

Even as a child, I looked at Christmas this way. I was looking forward to the meal, the sweets and, most of all, the smells of the season and the lights on the Christmas tree. The children were not allowed into the living room all day long. My father was dressing the Christmas tree in private. Mother was cooking. My parents couldn't make the day go fast enough for the children. Finally, the Christmas dinner of roasted pork and duck was served. We ate from the fine china that my mother had collected over the years. We chatted and had a really good time.

Dessert was always the same. I would venture a guess that 99% of all Danes have the same dessert on Christmas Eve. It's the best thing you have ever tasted. I still serve it every Christmas—sweet rice pudding with chopped almonds and lots of whipped cream. It is served cold with hot cherry sauce. In the very best Danish tradition, the pudding must have one whole almond hiding in it. The person who gets this almond gets the "almond gift." It was usually a cute pig made out of delicious Danish marzipan. I would eat until I got sick to my stomach but was usually rewarded with winning the "almond gift."

After dinner, my father would go into the living room and light the candles on the tree. He would then invite the family in with a proud nod. The children were super excited and couldn't say enough nice things about the tree. My father would hand out little Christmas hymnals, and we would each choose a song we wanted to sing. It was the only time we ever sang together as a family. It was magical, and I was high from being happy. Finally, after the singing, we would open our few Christmas gifts one at a time. We always had to wait for each other and never open at the same time. The opening of gifts then took a bit longer and was really more fun. I hated for the evening to end, even though it was my birthday the next day. I did compare my gifts with the gifts of my classmates. I can honestly say that I wasn't jealous. I so loved the atmosphere and the feeling of having a cozy time inside my own family. Why couldn't it always be this nice?

I do remember one bad Christmas. When I was a child and well into young adulthood, I suffered from urinary tract and bladder infections multiple times a year. They were severe, with bad fevers and peeing was very painful. My mother would usually wait to visit the doctor until I couldn't take the pain anymore—about a week or so. My mother hated doctors. She was embarrassed about her weight and, in general, fearful of any authority figure.

I remember walking to the bathroom doubled over in pain. She would walk next to me. She felt sorry for me but didn't do anything to help me. One December, when I was seven-years-old, the urinary tract infection was particular bad. It began as usual with pain while peeing and then went onto a very high fever. I could not find peace anywhere—standing, sitting or lying down. This went on and on for weeks. I can still remember being too weak to open my few birthday and Christmas gifts.

The entire Christmas was a big blur. I didn't want to drink anything...that made me go to the bathroom. The combination of too little liquid and the fever made me dehydrated. No one cared about that. This terrible pain had now lasted about a month. One day there was a knock on the front door. It was the upstairs neighbor who was very concerned about me. She came over to me with the most beautiful tray full of nuts and sweets. In the middle of the tray was a porcelain angel. The angel was actually a candlestick. There was a red candle in it, and it was lit. The woman smiled at me. She then turned to my mother and said, "If you don't call a doctor this instant, I will." I do not know how this woman knew about my illness. I thought that maybe her son had told her that I wasn't in school or out playing. I felt so special that day; somebody was standing up for me. It was a good feeling, and I still have the little porcelain angel. When I feel in deep need for some help from above, I will light her up. Wherever I have moved, she has come with me in my hand luggage. When I say that somebody was looking after me, I wasn't totally wrong.

Was my mother a mean, evil person? I don't think so. She was a very hardworking woman in an unhappy marriage, with a husband who was unavailable, unhelpful, unsupportive and often sarcastic and cruel. In her own weird way, I think she loved him. I think she was overwhelmed, tired and worn out. She never thought anything through; she just reacted to life. She took what little she could. There weren't many adults in her life, so she took from her own children. She took our affection—she didn't give affection. She took what she needed. I wasn't very old before I hated her kisses and hugs. They felt wrong. They didn't belong to me. I had already learned not to trust anybody, but I also began not to trust myself. I loved my mother, and I hated my mother; some days I hated her so much that it overwhelmed me.

Where do I go with this? It went into more fear, depression, and night terrors.

My mother's work was never done. When we were small, she cleaned houses with her small children in tow. When we were older, she would be up before dawn to make us breakfast and pack our school lunches...all this before she went to work as a cleaning lady. She did everything around the house. She did the shopping and the laundry, which was a huge task with the equipment available to her. Sometimes she would hang the laundry outside. I remember her hands being blue from hanging wet clothes in the frost. Sometimes the clothes were so frozen that they would stand by themselves. She also had to start the heating stove in the morning. In the winter, we often woke up with frost on top of our duvets. No one wanted to get out of bed, but my mother had to. First, she had to empty the ashes from the coal fire of the previous day. Then she carried them downstairs into the basement and filled a big bucket with coal and carried it upstairs. It was heavy work. Then she had to get the fire going. As my brother grew older, he became more and more involved with these tasks.

It took some time before the apartment defrosted. Mother worked long hours, and often the apartment was messy and in need of attention. I always thought that if I hurried up and vacuumed, she would be happy. If I dusted, she would be happy. If

I did the dishes, she would be happy. I tried to work as hard as I could. In the end, no matter how hard I tried, it didn't change anything. Sometimes she didn't even notice that I had cleaned the apartment "real nice" and that hurt my feelings.

SNIPPET EIGHT:
CRUELTY

My younger brother was born in 1965, in the cold month of January. When I was little more than six-years-old, I came home from school and was told to go outside and play. Aunt Lise was there with another woman—the midwife. Some hours later, I had a little brother. Aunt Lise stayed and made dinner for the hungry family, but the next morning my mother had to go about her chores as usual. I wished she could have realized that she was incredibly strong. She only had negative things to say about herself and anything else for that matter.

So now, we were six people in the small apartment. My brothers shared one bedroom and my sister, and I shared the other. My parents bought a sleep sofa for themselves and, from then on, they slept in the living room. My dad never got up in the morning until everything was done, including his late breakfast that was often four or five hours after we all had our breakfast. My mother's workday was well under way. My mother must have been annoyed with him, but I didn't know any better. All I remember was that we were not allowed to disturb dad and that he slept in the only room that had some good heat.

My lovely little brother was a handful, and my mother was out of control. She hit him a lot. I remember her hitting him so hard with a wooden shoe-horn that it broke. My brother had learned early not to cry. He would look up at her with indifference. She obviously thought that violence was the answer to controlling him. He stopped caring about her or anything else.

It was hard for me to watch and I remember wanting to be his mother—a caring one. Again, I took on way too much responsibility at a very young age. I would try to comfort him and be nice to him. He was angry, wild and very strong for his age. I looked after him when my mother went shopping or had other errands to run. I was a good six-years-older, but I could not control him. He would tie me to the bed and hit me with his toys. Then he would run outside. I had failed in my role as "babysitter." I hated it when he hit me, but I liked his spirit—the strength to dare to stand up for himself. When he got older, he would pick fights with much bigger boys. The beatings that he took at home had to "come out" somewhere.

One particular day stands out in my mind. My sister and I had been at the beach all day. As we arrived home on our bikes, we noticed a big fire truck and a police car in the parking area. *How exciting*! We ran upstairs to see if my mother knew what was happening. We had to take a big step back when we saw the police were sitting in our living room. My mother looked very pale and frightened. This was serious. My little five-year-old brother had found some matches and set fire to a big field planted with wheat. The whole field burned and my little brother was responsible. I thought he was going to be taken away, but we were left with a warning.

My mother always wondered why he was such an angry, uncontrollable boy. She spoke as if he was born that way. As usual, she didn't take responsibility for anything. He was trouble, but I loved him and didn't get too upset over his bad behavior. I knew in my gut that he would have stopped if someone had more time and understanding for him. He eventually stopped the bad stuff and became a very nice and calm man.

Where was my dad in all this? I can't remember. My mother once told me that she wouldn't let my dad hit us, as he didn't know when to stop. I didn't think that she controlled her anger towards my little brother very well. Obviously, she thought she was the lesser evil of the two. How did she know that my dad didn't know when to stop? Was my older brother correct when he assumed that my father had been tough with us when we were babies? I don't know, but my father always scared me.

My dad was a strange man, and I never could understand him. He was a tyrant, and everything had to be for his benefit, or it didn't matter. I have a hard time with the fact that he never helped his wife or his children. He didn't think it was his responsibility to feed or clothe his children. I don't know what his problems were but, according to my mother, he wasn't strong. So why didn't she just beat him up and ask for some help? The only time he was somewhat of a dad was when we became a little bit older. We could play cards or other games with him but only when he wanted to play. When we got good enough to beat him, the games stopped. He only loved to win and laugh at us.

I think he was lazy and totally irresponsible. I remember my older brother standing in the basement sawing wood for the stove using an enormous fretsaw. He was sawing for hours at a time until his little fingers had blisters. I would sometimes go downstairs to help him, but my chores were mainly upstairs. He alone was responsible for sawing wood in a cold and dark basement. He couldn't even reach the light switch, but he managed. Perhaps he found a stool. I can't remember that detail. Central heating was installed when he was about eight-years-old. Therefore, all the sawing that I can remember would have happened before he turned nine-years-old. It's almost inconceivable to look back onto those days and believe my own memories. My dad never saw any reason to make life easier for his family.

My dad loved to humiliate us, and he especially loved to put my older brother down. Even as a small girl, I would cry for my brother. It felt so unfair that my dad would blame my brother for his own failed life and having to marry mother. Whenever my brother had a hard time with a toy, schoolwork, or friends—*it could be any weakness*—my dad would go for the kill. I do not remember him being physically violent, but his sarcasm, humiliation, and shaming were so terrifying—I would rather have been beaten. My dad could look at you with such disgust in his eyes that you would crumble. He loved it when he could be big and strong and, just like my mother, he could only use his children. Who else would look up to him and find him fantastic? My father craved praise, and the children obeyed. He never dished out any praise to his family and he pretty much treated my mother as badly as his children. I didn't learn that women could stand up for themselves.

My dad made some cruel games for us. I remember being really small and my dad always had some sweet licorice rolls. He would eat these candies right in front of us. We were not allowed to have any of his candy. One time we asked if we could please have some licorice. He smiled and began to cut the sweet into minuscule pieces. Then, he threw the pieces on the floor. We had to eat the small pieces like animals. My dad had a great time being entertained by his stupid children. This is still humiliating to think about it—more than 50 years later.

Other times, he would ask me to shut up for an hour. If I could keep quiet for that long, he would give me 1 Krone. You could get a small ice cream for that amount of money. When the hour was almost up, he would begin to tickle me or angrily demand that I answer his questions. I don't remember ever getting any money, and I soon learned not to trust him or that idiotic game.

My mother would let us play all over the place; she didn't care if the apartment looked like a total mess. If dad was home, we could only play quiet games or run outside to play. Sometimes, on rainy days, when dad wasn't home, we would make a tent using the dining table. We would use blankets and clothespins and bring in pots and pans to play with. We would pretend to be on a camping trip. It was the closest we ever came to camping. As soon as we could hear the motorbike driving towards our home, we all stopped, looked at each other and frantically began to tidy up. It all had to be gone before dad covered the bike and climbed the stairs. My mother was just as nervous as we were and helped us as fast as she could and while also making sure that the food was ready when he walked in. My heart was pumping so fast. I was sure that he would throw me out of the apartment just as his stepmother had thrown him out. Or even worse—he often threatened to send me to an insane asylum, and you will never get out of this place. The insane people do terrible things to you, and you never see your family again.

I was little, and I believed him. Every time dad said, "I think I can hear the car coming—the car that is going to take you to the insane asylum." My soul would go into shock, and after a while, all he had to say was, "Listen I think…" He didn't have to say anymore, he would just look at me and see my reaction.

It obviously never happened, but I was deadly frightened during all my childhood years. To this day, whenever I am in an argument with my husband, friend or a total stranger, I can still get that sinking feeling of being unworthy and that somebody will throw me out or send me away, never to be seen again. This kind of thinking has always interfered with my life, especially as a teenager and a young woman. I didn't dare to be different from anybody and didn't dare to stand up for myself. I still have difficulties with disagreements and loud voices. My chameleon behavior came in very handy—but I lost myself. I am still working to find myself. *Maybe that's why I am writing this book.*

Before I was eight, I had begun to hunch over like an older person. I simply imploded and my shoulders moved inwards and downwards. I had a hunched and haunted look. One shoulder was getting lower than the other, and there was a real bend in my spine. At nine, I went to the hospital for a month. I do not know what they told my parents, but I was told I had a bad back and would have to live with it for the rest of my life. They gave me some exercises to do every day, but my family made fun of me when I did them. After a week or so, I never did them again. The back problem didn't have a name, according to my parents and we never really talked about it.

It was only much later in life that I realized that it had a name and that something could have been done early on. I went to a doctor in Switzerland, and she mentioned that I had bad scoliosis. She thought it was funny when I told her that I didn't know anything about scoliosis. I was so ashamed, and once again, I felt my parents had set me up. I often think the Danish healthcare system exists for the doctors and not for the patients. How could they have kept this away from me for so many years? It was always referred to as a bad back as if I was too stupid to understand the real word.

Doctors in Denmark often act like small kings and the patients are not important. A bad back was just another thing—*Suffer in silence, Kirsten.* It seems to me that nothing can be done about anything and I see the same attitude today with my niece and nephews. Coming to America was a bit of a shock. Everybody seems to know more about their bodies and diseases in general. Americans demand that something is done, or they go see another doctor. In Denmark, I wasn't even allowed to see my own files. These medical records belong to the state and not to me. I always had to go through my family doctor; it was like going to a gatekeeper. If he didn't think a specialist was needed, I didn't get one. I guess when the system pays the bills, you can't demand very much.

This incurable bad back was a big problem for me, and I was always hiding in big clothing. I never wore anything that would show my shoulders. I always hoped that something could be done and one day I learned about Alexander technique. It was around the time I moved to Switzerland. The Alexander Technique is a way to learn how to get rid of harmful tension in the body. It is a way to correct the posture, not from doing something but from un-doing tension. The technique teaches to find ease in movement and also a better understanding of how not to overuse the body. For example, it wasn't necessary to tense your shoulders to brush your teeth. The technique needed to be applied in every aspect of daily life. Always be mindful and stop when tension is felt. It sounds so easy, but it takes years to learn these new habits. I went to the same woman for many years, and I could still learn more. It was amazing to follow the changes that happened to me, slowly over time. My spine began to straighten, and my shoulders became less hunched over. My back pain went away. Later on, I worked in gyms, and I am almost as straight as anybody else. Only when I am really tired, do I hunch over. The first day with a strapless dress was a miracle for me.

TEEN IN TROUBLE

Peer pressure and the need to fit in put me on a sketchy road during my teens. I was not more than 13 years when I began to smoke and somewhere around 14 when alcohol was introduced to me. Drugs, especially pot, were available, but I was very scared of drugs. My dad had put the fear of drugs into me very young. It obviously worked. (I wished he had warned me about cigarettes and alcohol but that would have made him a hypocrite as he was using both.) In spite of the rumors and my own stories to hide behind, I have never tried any drugs. When peers would smoke pot, I would ask for a beer, and that worked. They stopped pestering me.

Drunkenness helped me with my shyness. It felt free and less intimidated by everything. Best of all, it took the edge off my night terrors. I finally fit in!

There were a couple of years when I just became a drunken teen amongst other drunken teens. I don't know if my parents noticed. I certainly have no memory of conversations with them about the abuse of alcohol and its effects. Fortunately for me, my older brother, who hated alcohol and was teased mercilessly for years about this, tried to drum some sense into my head. I used to hate his prosecuting eyes, but I think I would have drunk more had he not been there. Sometimes he would help me home and let me sneak to bed. He said good night to my parents. The next day he would give me an earful. It was hard to say no to my newly found peer group—the kids who thought that alcohol was wonderful.

It never occurred to me that drinking alcohol could be harmful to my health or that I could get into situations I couldn't handle. After all, I wasn't as drunk as the adults in my neighborhood, and I didn't drink every day. I was setting myself up for failure— smoking, drinking and hanging out with the wrong teens. I didn't think much about furthering my education or what I should do later in life. I was just trying to fit in and not hurt too much. As time went on, I began to see that other kids were heading for the gymnasium (high school), and a small wish began to emerge—to continue my education.

My parents didn't make it easy for me. My father didn't want me to be educated simply because it just wasn't done in our family. My mother was scared of educated people. My parents both believed that when you are born into a working-class family, you have to stay a working-class person. Why bother with an education? When my father was at home, I wasn't allowed to have enough space to do home-work...especially big projects. I didn't have a table in my little, shared bedroom. Homework was done at the coffee table or the dining table. In the win-ter, when my father hardly ever left the apartment, my papers would annoy him. I couldn't spread them out without being told to go somewhere else. There wasn't anywhere else. During the summer, when my father did do some work, I had a bit more room; but, as soon as I heard his motorcycle, I would begin to pack up. My mother, on the other hand, was ner-vous about upsetting my teachers if I didn't prepare for classes. Between the two of them, completing schoolwork was never easy. I did have a little hope for some higher education, but my parents were the ultimate decision-makers. I can honestly say that my parents and I never had a single conversation about my education or future.

I had one adult person I really looked up to and loved...my mother's half-sister Anna. She was a bit older than my mother and had many of the same low self-esteem problems as my mother. Aunt Anna was a lovely and caring person. She always had time for me, and I loved when she and her husband came to visit. They visited about once a month all throughout my childhood and teenage years. She had a quiet dignity about her and was always nicely dressed. She was in control of herself. People around her behaved better; they became calmer and less dysfunctional. Even her brother, my Uncle Alfred, didn't tell his awful stories when she was around. She just wouldn't take that kind of language. I do believe she had a good personal relationship with God. She was a churchgoer but didn't make a big deal out of it. She provided enormous help and support for my mother, and that meant that she helped me a lot too. When she was visiting, I could be a child. I loved her so much.

Every summer she and her husband invited me to their home for a week's vacation. It was heaven! They played games with me, and we went to the park together. They made me feel so safe and wanted. Aunt Anna made all the foods that I liked, and she taught me how to do needlepoint and knitting. She had time and patience, and I never felt like I had to hurry. I didn't have to worry about her being angry with me. Every single morning, her husband would go to the baker and buy me my favorite Danish pastry. I loved them both. The week came to an end much too fast.

I loved spending time with Aunt Anna and her husband. I especially loved my time with them in their summer house. They purchased a tiny, cute and super-cozy, wooden summer house near a Danish fjord. The sounds of birds were lovely, and my Aunt taught me the names of all of them. The smells of freshly cut grasses, fir trees and freshly picked berries hang in the air, together with the scent of the salt water from the fjord.

Aunt Anna would wake me up early so that we had a chance to watch the local wildlife. Deer, badgers and foxes loved the garden, especially early in the morning. My Aunt Anna and I would sit quietly and close together while waiting for something to happen. It was special to share these moments. After breakfast, we would go to the shallow beach to find "hole cows." Hole cows are stones that have moved back and forth in shallow water for a very long time. Slowly a grain of sand begins to make a hole in the stone and eventually a real hole is created. These holes are very rare, but my Aunt collected them on a long string. As a small child, I thought she was magical. She was also very good at finding four-leaf clovers, a skill I soon developed. We had so much fun together. My aunt and uncle didn't have a lot of money, but the time they spend with me was priceless.

Aunt Anna had such patience with me. Everything she ever taught me has become important in my life. I still do cross-stitch, needlepoint, bake and cook and, of course, I never pass a chance to find a four-leaf clover. It reminds me of her, and my heart is happy.

My uncle didn't say much. He did his own thing; I mainly saw him at mealtime. He was a firm but loving man. I felt safe around him. I knew he wouldn't humiliate and tease me.

It wasn't just me who loved to visit the summer house. There were always people coming and going. My Aunt Anna would be in the kitchen preparing all kinds of tasty things. She loved having people over, and they loved coming to visit. I wasn't accustomed to adults and children mingling and playing together. The rules of this summerhouse were different. We would all play badminton, soccer, darts, dice, cards and many more games. Even when visiting the summerhouse with my parents, we all did things together. I loved it. I would see a happy and playful part of my parents. My mother would sometimes play with us at home too, but my father never came outside to play. At the summer house, he could be fun and playful. He was actually a good athlete. Who would have guessed that? My mother relaxed and had fun. I loved to see her smile and laugh. Unfortunately, it didn't spill over into our life at home. Aunt Anna and her husband had a lovely way about them, and I will always be grateful for their love. As a child, I had one wish. I wanted Aunt Anna to move in next door, so my mother wouldn't be so unhappy.

When my son was born, I would take him to the summerhouse. It wasn't easy to get there by train, but

I wouldn't have missed it for the world. I loved seeing him running and having fun on the same grass that used to make me so happy. When Aunt Anna died about 20 years later, we lost somebody very special. Now the family had nowhere to go and have fun together. I miss her so much. It hurts.

Aunt Anna and her husband were the only adults who didn't seem to believe that there was something wrong with me. I always felt they genuinely liked me and, without them and their love, I would have been even more lost than I already was. At times, they even stood up for me, and that was a fantastic feeling. One episode stands out. I had finished my 10th grade with enough good grades to enter gymnasium (similar to high school in the US). My dad wouldn't let me go to further my education, but I was still going to the ceremony where they were giving out the diplomas. Aunt Anna and her husband were going to be there together with my parents. My aunt and uncle came first to my home, and together we would all go to the school. They were very formally dressed. I felt important. They cared about my graduation.

My mother and I were also dressed as nicely as possible, but my dad sat on the sofa in a pair of old work pants. "You can't go like that," my Uncle said. My dad looked at him and said, "I have never set foot in that school, and I don't plan to start today." My uncle responded, "Oh yes you are. You get your butt off that sofa and get dressed this very minute, or I will personally dress you and drag you to the ceremony." To my surprise, my dad didn't say anymore. He got dressed, and we all went together. It was a nice day. My mother had bought me a gift—a very nice silver bracelet. I still have it.

In my forties, I cut all ties to my parents. One reason involved Aunt Anna's death. One day, my mother called me in Switzerland and told me that Anna was dead. I wondered what happened and asked my mother, "Did she die in an accident?" It was such a surprise to me. I hadn't heard anything about her being sick. I was told she had been ill for a while and she had been in a hospital the last week or two. I demanded to know why I hadn't been told. My mother honestly told me that since I hadn't called her often enough, she was not going to pick up the phone and tell me about Aunt Anna. She was not telling me about her illness to teach me yet another lesson. *If I don't call or if I don't act as she wants me to, she will punish me.* The punishment was that I didn't have a chance to say goodbye to my beloved Aunt Anna. I was so sad and angry that I couldn't continue to speak to my mother and I had to hang up the phone.

It was hard for me to digest this behavior from my mother. I had always had excuses for her—she's depressed, she doesn't know any better, she has no support...blah, blah, blah. This time I felt that she was downright cruel and manipulating. The other sad part of the story was that no one from my extended family called and told me about Aunt Anna being so sick. That also hurt a lot.

I did go to Anna's funeral and cried like a small child. I had stopped seeing my sister about six months before this and the atmosphere was not pleasant. My parents stood around my sister as a shield. They were protecting her from the monster that I was. *How dare I have my own opinion and differ from the family's set of norms and fixed programming?*

During that time, my husband and I owned a small summer house in Denmark. I had bought it to be near my family and to have some connection to Denmark. It always felt so good to go there and speak my own language and to see all the things that I knew so well. After the ordeal of Anna's funeral, I decided to go ahead and sell the small house. I had had enough of Denmark. *Who am I kidding—thinking that my family and I could be normal together?* My husband was never attached to Denmark anyway. So, it was an easy decision. The house was sold quickly, and I have never regretted it.

WAKING UP TO ADULT LIFE

I t was hard to see my classmates go on with their higher education. There were only two girls that didn't continue in my class. I knew it was of no use to dream since; I had learned early that I was a second-class person. I was an uninformed teenager. I didn't know that in Denmark there were all kinds of assistance for people who wanted to study and didn't have the means. Education was actually free, but since my father didn't want to feed me, I would have had to go somewhere else to live and eat. I never knew that and didn't know where to go with my questions.

After tenth grade, I left school and began working for a dentist. I became a dental assistant, a very low paying job. I liked working there. I had to pay my parents for room and board, as did my brother. We thought it was just normal. Normal? My sister lived at home until she was almost 30-years-old and she never had to pay a penny. My brother and I had to rethink that family rule. By the way, somehow my sister wasn't second-class like the rest of the family. I never understood how that happened. I always knew that she had special rights in the family. My mother always felt it was our duty to take extra care of my sister. She always received much better gifts than her siblings and better clothes. My father thought it was funny when my sister badmouthed her siblings and her mother. He loved it and would laugh with her. She developed quite a tongue.

I know that I was no saint and surely hurt her at times, but her attitude towards me reached the point of no return. I have had no relationship with her for the past 20 years or so. When we meet at rare family events, we are polite to each other, but nothing more. I am not saying that my sister had an easy childhood. She had her problems and life wasn't easy for her. I am talking about the feeling that within the family she could say and do what she wanted. The same consequences were not put on her. No doubt that the warped thinking of our parents hurt her too. No one could leave this family system without deep scars.

It was during this phase of my life that I met my first husband. I was only 16-years-old, and he was about six-years older—so worldly and so adult. I was in heaven. Someone wanted me. I didn't stop and ask myself if he was the right person for me or if he was a good man. All I could see was that I was being given some kind of love. I was craving this love as a starving man craves a good steak. I had never received compliments. *This feels so good.* He invited me out and then paid for it! I didn't know people did that sort of thing. I was so naïve and overcome with gratitude to this person. He even said he loved me. I didn't think anybody could ever love me…I was unlovable. I fell for the whole thing—hook, line and sinker. We had a lot of fun and the weekend drinking went on and on. We moved in together and married the year after. I never realized how much we were drinking until I became pregnant when I was 20-years-old.

It was a bit young to be pregnant; none of my peers had babies. I tried to quit smoking but couldn't totally give it up. I hate myself for that to this day and still worry about what possible harm I did to my son. I did stop drinking. It was terrible to go to a bar or be with friends when I was sober. My old shyness and the less-than-others-feelings came back. I began to isolate myself more and more. My thinking became clearer, and I was beginning to grow up. I must have stopped growing up at 13-years- old and now had to catch up and pick it up in a hurry. I had to be an adult when the baby arrived. I did seven years of growing up in the first three to four months of my pregnancy. Sadly, my husband didn't grow with me. I began to see him differently and didn't like that I was seeing. I am sure that he didn't like what I had become either—a boring wife. He began to stay after work and have some beers with the boys. Our growing apart was already in the making.

I was about five months pregnant when I woke up one morning, and it was as if some enormous fog began to lift inside my brain. It was like seeing the world for the first time. I realized at that moment in my life that I had no idea who I was or what on earth I was doing being pregnant. I was sure that the thought of becoming a mother and the responsibility that comes with it brought about this new insight. It sounds like something wonderful happened to me, but this new sight brought me to my knees. I fell into a depression so deep that it lasted until my son was three-years-old or more. I woke up to the fact that I was with a man who was unavailable and unsupportive. He liked his beers way too much. I was doing what had been expected of me—mindlessly reliving my mother's sad life—blindfolded and brainwashed. I had become an unthinking puppet, and my mother loved it. Now we were the same; we could sit and be bitter together. For the first time ever, I realized that I could have a say in things and, if I dared, life could be different. I had always just done as expected and I had become addicted to pleasing everyone but myself.

I lived life as if someone was hunting me. I was always in survival mode. *Did my opinions count in the world? No, not even to myself.* I had stopped having any opinions. My needs were not important and never met. I had no dreams and ambitions for the future. I knew I was going to die young.

So, on that morning when the fog began to lift, I was literally slapped awake. I began to look at *my* responsibility in life...or lack thereof. I had given up without a fight. I believed the lie that I was second-class, and I blamed my parents for everything. I had not done for myself what I should have done...stand on my own two feet. It was the first time that I looked at myself and the word *pathetic* came to mind. It was the first time ever that I'd been real about my situation or myself. I began to hate myself even more. *What a coward I am!* I felt dead inside, and I was carrying another life inside me. I didn't know where to go with my questions. I felt utterly helpless, and my self-hate grew and grew. After about a month, I went into early labor and thought I was going to lose my baby. *Maybe the baby feels so unhappy inside me that the baby wants out of me—this angry person.* The doctors stopped the labor and, for the rest of the pregnancy, I was bed-ridden, with lots of time to think and chew on things.

"Breech birth," said the doctor and the C-section would be on July 20, 1979. *Did I go alone? I do not remember.* My husband surely wasn't there when I woke up. I had a little beautiful son—so pretty. I loved him on the spot. My parents came to see my new baby and me. Where was my husband...the new father? I was so happy with my new little baby, but I was worried something had happened to my husband. How could he not show up? He didn't show up until the next day and gave me some ridiculous reason for not coming. I stayed in the hospital for some days and enjoyed getting to know my little baby. When it became time to go home, no one came to pick us up. This time he was not missing, but he was late. He reminded me of my dad in his irresponsibility. Somebody had slashed the tires on our old used car, so he had taken the bus to the hospital. I couldn't believe people would do something like that and we spent our little money on a taxi home. Only a month later did the truth come out. When I was having the baby, my husband was out celebrating and drinking. On the way to visit me, he was stopped by the police for DWI (driving while intoxicated) and taken to the police station. They took his license away from him. When it was time to pick me up from the hospital, he slashed the tires on our car and made up a story, instead of telling me the truth. I learned about this when the mail came with a letter from the court system, and I had to sign for it. I never before opened anyone else's mail, but I had known for a time that something wasn't right. My husband was very scared by it all, but I was so angry with him lying to me that I frankly didn't give a damn. Yes! We had learned well. We didn't know how to be supportive adults for each other.

LETTER TO MY MOTHER (1995)

I wrote this letter to my mother after trying to make her understand my feelings and me. It was originally written in Danish. I have translated it, but I think it was more to the point in its original language. I have translated it almost word-for-word, and sometimes I repeat myself. I obviously wanted her to finally hear me. I never actually sent it to her. I didn't dare, and I didn't think she would have understood me anyway. I have kept it in my little secrets box for years.

Start of Letter

You obviously didn't understand one word of what I said to you the other day. Maybe I didn't express myself very well. Maybe I am still a coward, but I have to tell you what is real for me and what lies below the surface. Maybe I don't know it myself. It is easy to criticize a small situation that happened yesterday or to be mad over something that was said between my sister and me. I use these little examples as if they were the whole problem. I can't find words for the more difficult stuff including my emotions or lack of them and the not-allowed emotions or the wrong emotions.

I can't stop the feeling that I have been abandoned, put aside and wronged. I am not like other people. These are emotions that have been with me forever. I have not been loved for being the person I am. I have always had to put myself last. I have learned it would be egotistical to do something for myself. "Mother doesn't like you when you behave in such-and-such a way. You are not allowed to think or feel these things. You are wrong, and your behavior is wrong."

I always had to take special care not to hurt your feelings. Mother will be sad if you... I can fill in the blank with practically anything. I am now asking you this question. *How can a child make her adult mother sad?* Mother is getting a headache or mother starts to cry. So, I tiptoed around you, tried not to be me but a copy of you. You couldn't see the difference between us anyway. You were ashamed of things I said or did as a child. You couldn't accept that I was an individual person with my own thoughts, my ideas and my own personality.

When I finally learned to become a clone of you and learned to live your way, I had to accept a life where I was made responsible for your emotions, your life, your problems and your sadness. It was up to me to make you happy. I will not and cannot take responsibility for your life, your sad marriage and unhappy childhood or for your lack of love from your husband. It is not my fault that you have no sex life and it is not up to me to be the surrogate husband. I always felt that your kisses and caresses were repulsive because they were not meant for me, but for another adult. I felt this in my gut...strong sexual undertones. I didn't understand it then, but now there is no doubt in my mind.

I couldn't say no or push you away. I didn't even know that a mother shouldn't behave like this. Through the years, your advances became more and more unbearable. You stole the love you needed from me and, at the same time, you ruined my understanding of love and what it means to be sexual. To this day, I have a hard time when I get a hug. My body stiffens and can't relax. I would have loved to be able to say no to you. But how? All children need tons of love and affection, but it should be given without shame and always without condition. I was in great need for affection and took what I could get, but if I had told you how I felt about it all, you would have started to cry. Then it would be up to me to make you happy again. I was between a rock and a hard place. How you came to the conclusion that it was up to me—a child—to be responsible for you is beyond me. It should have been the other way around. In my family, everything got turned upside down.

The children were blamed for the emotions of the parents. The only emotions allowed were their emotions, and we could no longer feel our own. My emotions were put aside. I feared being shamed. It was hard to be a child while being your protector and giving you happiness and joy. Children can't give these kinds of presents. Children are the presents in life, and they deserve understanding and forgiveness. Love should never be withheld, even if the child does or says something stupid.

We are not allowed to be noisy because that will make dad angry. We are not allowed to be noisy because it will irritate the neighbors. We are not allowed to be loud because mother will get a headache. I was not allowed to be heard and that has stayed with me to this day. I still have a difficult time listening to music, singing, screaming out loud—or just a small thing like cutting the grass. I worry about what the neighbors might think. *Am I a nuisance?*

This was a constant threat in our house—this "what will the neighbors think." They could be loud, sing and scream, but I was not allowed to do the same. "You, little Kirsten, are nobody and don't you ever think you will amount to anything. Don't you ever think you are smart, intelligent, pretty or just as other people because you are not. My children are nobodies. Don't ever dare to think you can have an education. You are my daughter, and we are stupid and shall always remain stupid. Become like your mother—do not have ambitions. Stay where you belong—the lowest in all things."

The message was clear. You will only help me if I am even more pathetic and helpless than you. Don't you ever think that you are more than I am. I know exactly what you are thinking. *Imagine how terrifying it is to believe that your mother can read your mind.* If this is true, there is no place to hide, and nothing is private— no dreams or fantasies. You didn't like dreams and fantasies anyway. Life is not made to dream...life is without hope. When your innermost thoughts can't be secret, life is dangerous. For years I believed that you knew what I thought, even if we were far away from each other. Again, it is a total lack of reality. You believe that I am you and refuse to face the fact that I have thoughts of my own. It's not surprising that I was paralyzed and incapable of anything. "I am only there for you if you are 100% like me. If not, then no help, no new clothes, no food, no, no, nothing. It was cruel, and even though somewhere deep inside I knew you were wrong, I didn't dare take the chance and be me. What if I died from it?

I AM NO LONGER AMONG THE LIVING. I AM THE LIVING DEAD. YOU DEMAND THAT I FEEL SORRY FOR YOU?

You and dad never allowed me to study. Dad didn't want to feed me for that long. "Why do you think you have two hands? Go out and work so you can move out of the house sooner, rather than later." When I was sick, I had to be almost dead before I could see a doctor. I had to suffer with painful teeth, even though both doctors and dentists were free for children.

I had to guess everything...no explanations on anything. How does the radio work? Where do children come from? How do I use a public bathroom? What is menstruation? Thousands of questions and sometimes I guessed right, and sometimes I didn't. There was never any help unless I was pathetic. *Oh, poor little girl, you have a fever, but no doctor. Oh, poor little girl, you look so sad, but no understanding. Are you angry? Well, that is forbidden. But you mother...you could take what you wanted—my thoughts, my sexuality and my childhood.*

You took my life—who am I.

I wish to be me, and not that quiet girl who always pretends to be happy—who always understands and is never angry. Kirsten, who never demands anything and always does as she is told. I want to be *me* so badly that I don't care if you don't like me anymore. When you live like someone else, a puppet for you and only playing your roles, then you are dead.

"You don't speak out or take any space. You don't laugh spontaneously and learn to accept bad behaviors and violence in others. You never say no. You know where you belong—among the lowest. You don't get an education. You marry a man who drinks too much, and you pretend everything is just fine. That's just life and happiness is equal to sinning. And if by chance you should begin to feel happy, then quickly sit down and wait; it will not last."

I no longer feel the need to feel sorry for you or to listen to your complaints and negative hopes for the future. I no longer feel the need to smile without being happy, and I don't want to be anybody but myself. I know that I am a decent person and I no longer want to see myself as second-class. I am God's child and have as much right to be in this world as anybody else. I want to be somebody, speak my opinion and go into an expensive restaurant without feeling like a thief in the night.

We were the children, and you were the adult—just trying to clarify that to you.

I am beginning to find myself and all of a sudden I have thoughts you don't know. I behave differently, and that is shaking you to the core. You thought that I would always be thankful and grateful to you for "all that you did for me," and that I should be looking after you for the rest of my life. You make yourself pathetic and undeserving of other people's respect. What you haven't understood is that it is you who have to live your life and your children will not and cannot save you and live your life for you. If you would let me live my life, without wasting all your energy trying to change me, maybe there would be a little time to do something about your own life. If you feel that your life has gone past you, then it is your own fault. Of course, it is a shame but not my fault. And believe me, I tried to save you. I tried everything for years. If only I could do better, be somebody else, then my mother would finally be happy. What a huge misunderstanding I have had to live with for so long. I know now that I was born into a bad situation and I was not the one creating it. If you become sad over something I do or ashamed over something I say, then it is something you choose to be. You could also choose to be proud of your daughter, but that is probably asking for too much.

In your letter to me, you said that I don't care for the family and you get that impression from the fact that I have stopped calling, writing and visiting you. Can I take this opportunity to remind you that you are not my whole family? You are one person in the family. I can see the rest of the family even if I never saw you again. It is so frustrating—how you turn everything upside down.

How do you think it was for a child to know that mother and dad lived a loveless marriage? To know that you really didn't want us children and you didn't even try to hide that fact? To know that it was our fault that you had to stay married? To know that everything emotional was forbidden? To know that dad's family had a strange disease but not to know what it was? To know that my mother fears all human contact? To know that dad is weird? To know I wasn't allowed to have any success? Then I would be like all the people you were so afraid of…those who turned you into a second-class citizen. To know that our neighbors were severe alcoholics or child and sex abusers? We had to be quiet for these people? To know all this and not to be able to ask any questions is to make the world a very threatening place.

You didn't care if you scared us to death. I remember vividly the many times that dad didn't come home until past dinner time and every time you thought he was dead. Every time it happened, you stood staring out of the window. You would voice your fear to us…your small children. I begin to think that dad has had a motorbike accident and he is lying dead in the street somewhere. What am I to do? I can't feed you all and what shall become of me. Every time I thought you were right. How could I not believe my own mother? I saw the terror and tears in your eyes and thought we were all going to die. When mother is scared, so are the children. The small children who would say, "No need to be afraid, he will be here soon." We then would walk around the apartment, whispering in fear. Everything became surreal. There were days when he wouldn't come home until after our bedtime. We were in bed, but we knew mother would be standing at the window worrying about her future. It was always up to us to save you from everything. It is very heavy to carry your mother. Can't tell her anything, as she is too fragile. It's a world upside down as usual.

I really do think it is sad you have had such an unhappy life. My anger is about you making me believe that it was my fault and I had to do something about it. Children love their parents and will do anything possible to make the parents happy. In our family, that fact was used to the extreme. I still hunger for my parent's eyes that would look at me with pride, love and happiness. I hunger for someone saying that I am good enough—not great—just good enough.

To complete the sadness, we had a dad who in no way protected, cared for or tried to understand us. There was no help from him, and we could never count on him. We didn't know if he would come home at night or not or if he cared to speak to us or not.

I can hear him saying things like "shut up or go outside to play and stay away for as long as possible. Don't behave in any way that annoys me." Sarcasm and irony were his weapons. Small children didn't understand sarcasm and believed that everything was true. Dad loved it when we looked up to him. He loved it when we thought he was super smart. He expected our praise and pride instead of giving any to us. Again, a world turned upside down.

Dad had no feelings of responsibility and no ambition to live better than we were living already. "I had nothing as a child; therefore, you shall have nothing as well." And you mother...you ask me why I don't speak to dad. *I don't know him, and now I don't care to know him.* He thought that children were a kind of toy you could use or not use, caress or not, talk to or not, and then throw them away when they weren't funny anymore.

Today you expect me to be sweet and understanding and to have respect for dad. He never did anything for me. He never set foot inside the school. He never witnessed any part of my life. I would have loved to have a dad who was proud of me, but that never happened. It is as if he believed that if he gave praise, then he couldn't receive any. His lack of interest and absence of smiles still haunt my insides. He laughed at my naivety and looked at me as if I was one big joke. He had the audience that he craved as long as I stayed unknowledgeable and stupid. In my opinion, this was an abuse of children. It's just more than my brain could hold—letting your children stay dumb and not explain anything so that he could be entertained. I have waited for his interest since I was a little girl. It is an evil dream, and I continue to wait for some attention. But it will never happen, as he is the only one who is allowed to have any. He sits there on his throne as if he had been staging the whole thing; it's eerie. Imaging to wish for so little for yourself, your wife and your children?

When I was visiting last summer, I got a strange feeling in my belly. *She can't see me.* You mention that you miss the little girl I used to be—the happy girl as you called her, the girl who didn't know herself and smiled while crying on the inside. The girl I used to be when I didn't know who I was. You can't see the adult woman who is no longer addicted to you—a woman who dares to speak her truth, my truth as I see it. Of course, you miss the old Kirsten who never stood up for herself, who had no emotions, and who didn't demand anything at all. She doesn't exist anymore—this little girl, the doll with no will power, the girl who was so scared that she could hardly breathe.

I observed another strange behavior last summer. *She can't hear me.* You and I were talking about difficult things. I am trying to explain why I don't feel like visiting you anymore. I always feel that doomsday is near when I visit, and I will no longer tolerate that feeling in my life. There is falseness about everything. We smile, but there is no truth behind the smiles. I never dare to tell about positive experiences in my life. I remember telling you that I had just been to Paris, and you just replied, "What is all that traveling good for? Can't you stay home like normal people?" I mentioned that my son was doing great in his new school in Switzerland and as usual you can't say anything nice. "Yeah, it's always easier to get good grades when you have money." As if we were buying his efforts. Every effort to communicate gets hacked down. If the conversation is about something sad, then it is allowed to flourish.

While you and I were talking, I became more and more aware of the fact that my father never said a word...not one single word. As always, he had no interest in me. He couldn't care less if I came to visit or not. He didn't show any sign of emotions when I said goodbye. This reopened huge wounds in me. I got that old feeling as he looked at me. I started the old rant inside my head...you are unwanted, he didn't want any children, he didn't have any interest in you, and he thinks that I ruined his life. It is as if he wants to punish us for being born. Imagine the pain of never hearing your parents say that you are wonderful and that your mother and father love you. You are as you are and we love you. It is a longing I have, but if you said it to me today, it would be too late. I wouldn't believe you anyway.

It's a sad story, and it has to end. I insist on being happy, and I will find a way to be so.

End of Letter

I was surprised at how much anger I felt when I read this letter after so many years stashed away in a box. I always believed that I didn't know how to be angry. But of course, I didn't dare send it. Maybe it was best that way. It helped me a lot to write it, but I am not so sure it would have made any difference to my parents, assuming they had read it. But it did surprise me to see how much I actually knew about the roots of my emotional problems. I guess I knew these problems when I got mad enough and dared to see what I had not really wanted to see before. My problems for the future were about what to do and how I can change. How will people around me react to change? Obviously, my parents did not like the real me. They wanted the old false me back.

After writing the letter, I didn't see my parents for many years, except for a funeral and a confirmation in the family. It was the second time in my life I had stopped all contact with them. The first time was only for a couple of months, but this time I had really had my fill. I felt very guilty about not seeing them, but I knew that being around them would have made it impossible to do the work I needed to do. I would send them a Christmas card, and that was it. No more contact. At times, I missed them, but I did not miss the dysfunction. I missed what should have been a real family. They had helped me a lot with my son when he was little, and I felt that I owed them for that and that I had to be nicer. I was often torn. Was I being a revengeful daughter or was this really necessary for me to grow? I remember once I was visiting Denmark and driving through my old neighborhood. All of a sudden I saw my mother walking down the street. My heart stopped, and instantly my inner children were running wild. I felt a mixture of being scared and in need of my mother. I didn't know what to do. I continued to drive, and it has haunted me ever since. How could I have done that?

My dad died, and I didn't know whether I should go to the funeral or not. My mother told me not to come, as it would ruin her day. I ended up going. I do not know why I went. I thought it was expected of me, or maybe I went just to spite her. I honestly don't know. It was one of the worst days of my life. It was pretty much me against the family. My sister refused to speak to me or to shake my hand. I knew it would be a difficult day. I think I would have stayed home in Switzerland if I had known how bad it really would be. The message was clear. If you break any family rules, you are on your own. My older brother and I had found each other some years back. We were both going through some therapy and had begun to speak in a way that would have been impossible earlier in our lives. We had each other that day, and I couldn't have done it without him. My little brother tried to be neutral, but if he spoke to me, my sister would not speak to him. An old aunt told me to behave properly and be a bit more respectful. Maybe she was right about that. I had landed in Denmark the evening before. I was to pick up my older brother and then drive to the funeral.

I couldn't drive. My foot would not press down on the gas pedal. I swear to God this is true. It took me forever to drive the short distance, and we were running out of time. We finally arrived, and the funeral was just beginning. It certainly didn't look good to have the two first-born children walking up the aisle after everybody else had arrived. I was very embarrassed and hurried up and gave my mother a hug (a hug a felt I had to give), said hello to the pastor, tried to say hello to my sister but she was not in the mood. I didn't know what to do or where to sit, so I walked down and sat next to a cousin of mine. I did not sit with my immediate family, and that was ok with me—weird, but ok.

After the ceremony, we all went and had coffee. I should have left before that, but I survived. The hoops my sister had to go through—not to sit near or next to me and be in charge over who could talk to me—were almost humorous. My mother felt visibly uncomfortable about the whole affair. She felt guilty that I had been left out of a dinner the night of the funeral, a dinner in my mother's apartment for just her two youngest children and grandchildren. I remember my mother sneaking over to talk to me. It was a weird feeling; we hadn't spoken for years. She was asking my forgiveness for not inviting me. I felt so strange and all my old feeling of rescuing her surfaces. I stayed calm and told her that I was capable of finding my own dinner. I was very happy to leave the country.

Over the years, I often wondered if I would go to Denmark when my mother died. Then one day I got the phone call. She had a stroke and passed away. While thinking about what to do, my grandson made the decision for me. A few hours after the news about my mother, my son called and told me, that his wife had gone into labor a month earlier than expected. My first and only grandson was born on the same day my mother died. It was a crazy emotional day. My grandson made it easy for me. Of course, I went to see him, and he was the loveliest little boy I have ever seen. The best feeling ever is being a grandmother.

SNIPPET TWELVE:
THINKING ALOUD

Here is a new way of thinking for me. When I think that I am fundamentally flawed and that there is something wrong with me, I take everything people say to heart and get hurt very easily. I am beginning to learn that it is in my own thinking that I differ from other people and not necessarily their view of me. It's a new and discomforting angle for me to understand. I do believe that when I scream and brutalize myself in my head, it doesn't take a lot of comments from others to make me fall apart...total negative overload. These comments are not necessarily super-hurtful but heaped on top of my own low self-esteem and self-hate they grow out of proportion. If I had a strong core and inner belief of my own worth, the comments and judgments of others would have no meaning and would not be able to shake me. Without that strong core and inner strength, the world tumbles very easily. The thought that I was somehow to blame for my own hurt...not a pleasant feeling. The more that I look at those feelings, the more I realize that this is the case. I wish I had had some of that insight at the day of my dad's funeral.

All the enormous negative chatter in my brain was deafening. I always felt that I had to justify myself. I had to explain why I did and said things, just in case the person I was with at that moment didn't like it or disagreed with me. I have a hard time trusting my own right-to-be and do whatever I choose. The "new me" tries not to please everybody at all times. Slowly it is becoming more acceptable to me that some folks might not like me, and that I can live with that. I do not have to change my way of thinking or doing, and it doesn't make me wrong or bad. This is very new to me, and I am still on baby steps. First, I had to acknowledge the fact that I was addicted to pleasing everybody for obvious reasons. *You might die if you don't.* The second step was to dare little by little—try it out on my husband and other people close to me. I had to try first to make sure that the world wouldn't stop and that I was still in one piece. There are days it works better than others. I always thought that to be an assertive person you had to be yelling and screaming—maybe even hurt people.

That didn't work for me because of fear of my own anger. It was an anger that had been pushed so far down for so long that I was afraid it would erupt like a volcano and send destructions in all directions. I am slowly seeing that I can be strong in a nice, quiet way. There is no need to fight. I had to just say "no" and mean it firmly in the newly discovered core. When I trust myself and believe in my rights, it seems to me that the world lets me have it my way. I thought that I had to fight for everything I wanted or needed and since I didn't know how I went without. I am beginning to ask and set rules and boundaries for myself without any yelling. It sounds so easy, and it is that easy on the days it works. As soon as my old pattern of thinking and behaving creeps up on me, my fears come with them, and I begin to deny myself again. It is hard to change a lifetime of habits, but it is so wonderful when it works. With practice comes perfection.

I remember a funny story about how people react to you differently when you change. In Denmark, I had always felt very inadequate. Being a single mother after my divorce didn't make life easier and I hardly had any contact with other adults. I didn't mingle with the parents of my son's classmates. I felt they all looked down at me, just as I did. I tried to make myself as invisible as possible, and my eating disorder helped a lot. I was skinny as a rail. What a

pathetic, sad person I must have been! I did, however, have a little contact with one mother since our
boys played together.

After moving to Switzerland, the boy from my
son's class visited us many times. When we visited
Denmark in the summers, we would meet up with this
boy and his parents, and we became good friends. I
changed a lot in Switzerland. I gained a lot of weight
and began the journey of healing. Many years went
by and one day we were invited to a party with these
friends. It was a big party with a lot of people attend-
ing. I sat next to a woman who I knew as one of the
mothers from my son's old class. We were laughing
and having a great time. After a while, she said to
me. "It's so funny. You speak to me as if you know me
and I have never met you before." I smiled and told
her that of course she knew me, my son used to go to
school with her son before we moved to Switzerland.
She looked at me with disbelief in her eyes and said.
"I can't believe you are the same person. You used to
be this little sad, haunted woman. Congratulations.
I love the new you."

What a boost to my ego, I knew I was on the
right track. It had been a big step to dare to leave
my country with an 11-year-old boy, but I was reap-
ing the fruits. I still remember the day we moved
from Denmark. As we were sitting in the airplane
on the way to Switzerland, teary-eyed from leaving

our country, I said to my son. "Always remember that in Switzerland, no one knows us and we can change everything. This is our chance to create a new life for ourselves."

SINKING

I think my eating disorder was formed the day I woke up from *The Fog*. While pregnant, I tried to eat "normal," healthy foods but real hunger... I didn't have. During the entire pregnancy, I only gained about 10 pounds. When I came home from the hospital with my baby, I noticed a change in my attitude towards food. I simply didn't deserve it. It was somewhat "okay" to eat while breastfeeding but I didn't eat enough and pounds began to melt off me. Slowly over the next year, it grew into a real eating disorder. I would deny myself food but never deny my son. When I was home alone, I could go days without eating or just eating tiny, little bits. I was punishing myself for many things—maybe for everything. After my divorce, my ex-husband had my son every second weekend, and I hated it. My son wasn't happy, and he was often sick. It was tearing me apart inside, but the law was the law. When my son was at home, I always cooked meals. On the weekends, with absolutely no one around, it was heaven for an eating disorder.

My family began to notice that there was a problem. I denied it. My weight got to around 110 pounds and my periods stopped. My physical body began to fall apart, but emotionally, I loved it. It fit my mood, and I didn't deserve any better. The flu would find me several times a year, and colds and coughs became normal. My cigarette smoking certainly wasn't helping. Pneumonia, fatigue and caring for a kid— my life was utter chaos. Sleep never came to me. Honestly, I do not know how I survived. I didn't have any real jobs, and I couldn't make ends meet.

I had to stoop down and go to the social services. It was a hard day to admit that I was not just a failure but also a loser. I told social services about my situation and asked if there was any way that they could help for a while; thankfully they did. They helped me with my rent and general expenses while I went to school and got some more education. I needed this schooling to make enough money to feed my son and myself.

After a while, I began to work part-time, study part-time and do homework in the evenings. I worked really hard and did quite well. I remember sitting at an exam during the first day out of bed from pneumonia. I was at my lowest weight ever. Craziness! I passed with flying colors. Soon I was applying for jobs—general office work and bookkeeping. I also added English to my resume! I had English in school, as do all Danish kids. I learned the basics and could speak somewhat, but I never got good at it. My English reading and writing were extremely poor. I felt it was important and I began to read a lot of English books, dictionary in hand. I also found a few foreign friends who spoke English with me. I always did better around foreigners; I didn't feel as judged by them. They didn't know all the unwritten, cultural and social "rules of the Danes." My English was coming along very nicely, and I felt good about it. *Something to feel good about— WOW!* So finally, with my son in daycare, I began to work full time.

Life was still in chaos, and I had less and less time for my son. The old friend guilt was lurking as usual. I didn't have a driving license and couldn't afford a car anyway. Commuting was eating up precious time. I felt I should have been with my son when I was at work and felt that I needed to do work when I was with my son. My guilt grew to craziness. It was my fault that people were starving in Africa, my fault that people were sad or sick and my fault that milk was expensive. I had to run a little faster and hide behind a smile, which had become more and more forced. There was no more life in me and yet

I climbed out of bed every morning from a sleepless night. I cried a lot.

YES—I had done it. I became my mother.

I was just as overwhelmed and unavailable to my son as my mother had been to me. Of course, I knew my son needed a better mother, but I had no energy. I didn't know how to climb out from this sad place called depression. I just slowly sank. I knew I was sinking and I could do absolutely nothing about it. On the weekend, I tried to get some sleep and, since daytime sleep wasn't as frightening, I did get some rest. There were also chores such as laundry, shopping, cleaning, and cooking and baking. These activities became a weekly affair as my son was developing allergies.

I couldn't explain to my son why he had to go away every second weekend. He was just a little toddler. I couldn't explain what depression was—not even to myself. I thought I was just a lousy person who couldn't pull herself together. My son wasn't emotionally thriving…that was for sure. *Poor little guy.* It was—as always—my fault. Guilt and more guilt, and I was drowning in guilt. Days, weeks, even years went by. In those years, I had many jobs; but, as mentioned earlier, I couldn't keep my jobs.

I never had a hard time finding a new job, but the stress of being fired again was always on my mind, creating a nervous knot in my stomach. *I don't fit in.* I knew I was different. I also knew that a single woman with a child wasn't an employer's favorite person to hire and the old rule of "last hired first fired" didn't help me either. The self-hate continued. *You, Kirsten, are a bad mother! You can't keep a job. You don't even know how to sleep. You are bent over like an old woman. Everybody looks down at you.* I was hurting badly. I feared people around me and didn't speak very much. I kept to myself.

I remember vividly one time when a woman, a parent from my son's daycare was desperately looking for a babysitter for her daughter. There was a crisis in her family, and she and her husband had to go away urgently for the weekend. She was asking every parent who came through the door to the daycare if they could look after their daughter. I was standing there gathering my son's things. I turned to her and said that I would be happy to look after her little girl for the weekend. She looked at me with such horror in her eyes as if to say, "How dare you come near my child?" She was a little more diplomatic but not much. I felt like a mass murderer. I was so humiliated in front of other parents, and my soul was bleeding. I went home, and instead of cooking dinner I collapsed in tears. It was visible! People could see my unworthiness, and they even thought I would harm their children. It was a very long and sad weekend. My son wanted to play, but I couldn't be there for him. Again, I failed him and had failed myself too.

In the early years after the divorce, I saw my parents a lot. They were almost the only human contact that I had. I always felt that they genuinely cared for my son. They were nice to him, but they still had their rules, and it was difficult for me to protect my son from their old ideas about children. They were in control of me, and I often regressed back into childhood around them. My mother loved to have me around so she could share her fears and worries with me. Just as in childhood, she was overwhelming me with her needs. Her fears were contagious. My mother would call me every night after dinner, and we would have our usual bitter talk about how much life sucked. When she had had her fill of negativity, she would remind me, not just once but every single day, that it was a dangerous world and not safe to live alone. *Are the windows and doors locked? Remember to close the curtains so that the bad people can't see you.*

It is time to get scared. I didn't really need help in that department, but my mother pretty much paralyzed me each and every night. I became so paranoid that I would check the doors and windows, under the bed, the wardrobe—whichever place was big enough for a small person. Then I would check it all again. Over time, even drawers had to be opened. In the end, it didn't matter how much I checked because I knew that the horrific being that I feared could go straight through the wall. My night terrors were now beginning even before bedtime. I tried everything I could think of so that my son would not notice my fears. I am sure that I failed there as well.

So yes! My parents did help me in many ways. They were there to help with practical things and with my son. They also helped to keep me in the sick *Soup*—the quicksand. The more I wanted out, the deeper I sunk into it. It is hard for me to really describe how it was in those days. It was the deepest hopelessness than anyone could imagine. The sadder that I became, the less I allowed myself any food.

HOW BAD CAN IT GET?

I t kept coming. My father got into a habit of visiting me when I came home from work. The daycare closed at 5:00 pm and often I would just make it in time. I would then hurry home to begin dinner, get some food into my son and attempt to have a little fun time with him before his early bedtime. Often my dad would be waiting for me at my doorstep, and my heart would sink. *Now I had to entertain him, make coffee or serve him a beer.* My father demanded my full attention and my son would sit and wait—hungry, tired, and in need of a bath and some mother time. I was so torn between the two, but my father had the winning hand. He knew I was scared of him and couldn't stand up to him. So, he would just sit around for an hour or two and my tiny little window of time would evaporate, and my stress levels would grow to enormous proportions.

One day my son was lying on the floor crying and wanting his mother, and I finally told my dad that I had things to do and my son needed my care. My father had a way of looking at me like I was a piece of garbage and I crumbled into a three-year-old child. After a while, my son fell asleep on the floor without dinner. I was devastated and told my dad that I didn't think it was a good idea for him to come around on workdays. Clearly, he could see my son's needs weren't being met. My father didn't care one bit. As usual, it was only my father's needs that were important. I kept on talking about my son's lack of a bath and dinner. My dad looked at me and said, "Can't you talk about anything else but that kid? You have nothing else on your mind, so you obviously do not know how to live your life. You are a failure."

I told him that frankly I was lost and didn't know what to do. I thought that maybe I had a listening father after all. He said, "Well if it is that bad, why don't you kill yourself?" Shocked I said, 'But I have a son who needs me." He responded, "You can always take him first." I got up from my chair and, for the first time in my life, I threw my father out of my home. "Get out of my apartment and don't come back." He smiled and said that he would like to stay for dinner if I ever got around to making it. I repeated, "Get out! Get out!" When he was finally out the door, I collapsed on the floor and didn't know what emotion to feel. I screamed, cried, laughed and, for a moment thought, I would go insane.

He was finally going to get me into the insane asylum. After a while, I was exhausted and walked into the kitchen. I took a big cooking knife and thought about my life. Then I scared myself, called a neighbor and asked if she could come urgently as I was in danger. My son woke up and was hungry and fortunately my neighbor took care of him and called her husband, who took me to a hospital hoping to get something to calm me down. In the hospital, they locked me in a room for a long time. I was so angry that I overturned the furniture. I wanted out. I wanted my cigarettes. I wanted help. I was locked in like a criminal. I was ignored, and I met a rage deep down my stomach that I had never known before this. I screamed at God and the angels. I had never been a churchgoer and didn't consider myself spiritual. What was the use of having a Higher Power who would let you down and have people suffer?

On that day, I had reached rock bottom. My relationship with the angels had begun for real. I can't explain it, but slowly I came to believe that somebody out there was looking after me. That was the only explanation for my survival. My spirituality has grown over the years, and today I am fully convinced that without my belief in a higher power, I wouldn't have made it. After a long time, the doctor came in and asked how I was feeling. I told him that I was fine. I wanted him to send me home, and he did. End of story.

I can't believe it even to this day. I was in danger of hurting my child and myself. The doctor didn't care. He gave me nothing, and there was no follow-up appointment. I felt as though the doctor hadn't taken me seriously and that I wasn't worth his time. I was not worthy of care even at a moment of great need. I felt like the whole world had abandoned me. My neighbor drove me home. I picked up my child, and we went downstairs to our home. I put my son to bed. I sat for a long time, with all life beaten out of me. After the birth of my son, I rarely had any alcohol at all. I wished I had had something strong in the house that night.

This was the deepest hole I had ever climbed out of. It was also the time when I began to see that I had to learn to live a life without dependence on two dysfunctional and abusive parents. I decided not to see them for a while and not to ask for any help. If I had to work overtime, I would have to find other solutions. At that time in my life, I didn't really have friends. My parents were the only buffer between me and total loneliness. Things had to change. The price for needing them and being dependent on them was too big.

My mother called later that evening. "I can't believe you would throw your dad out of your apartment. How dare you?" I told her I was going to take a break from them for a while. I had come to the conclusion that it is never good when your parents know what you are doing every second of every single day. This was the first time in my life that I stopped seeing them and said no to them. I knew I had become their little child again and there was no growing in this trap—a trap set and lived by all three of us. Today I can certainly see my part in it—but at that moment in time—I had only one thought…get away from the monsters. *But* my depression was always there.

DEPRESSION AND LIES

What is depression? Does the same twisted thinking always cause it for everybody or is it different from person to person? I do not have the answer. It has been a longtime companion of mine, and it was often debilitating and at other times just a whisper. It was always there. The more I understand the dynamic behind it, the better I get. I do not believe that my depression is an illness. If I go see a doctor, I am always asked if I have ever suffered from any mental illnesses or depression. They often lump them together.

I wonder if they—"the famous they"—believe that depression is an illness. I get so mad, and I always answer, "No." It's none of their business that I get depressed more often than others. I hate their labels and the box it puts me in. I am not making light of people with any type of severe clinical depression. I am just sharing my thoughts and feelings. I would never discourage anyone from seeking the help that they need.

It is also worrying not to know where or to whom this information is going. Maybe they want it to be an illness so they can prescribe tons of medications? These are drugs that numb all the feelings so that you don't have to deal with them. I did take anti-depression medication at one time. It was when my son was real little, and I couldn't cope at all. I took those terrible pills with all their side effects for about eight months. Then I threw them out, much to my doctor's horror. I am not saying that medication is never right and should never be taken. I am fully aware that certain illnesses required daily medication. For me, pills didn't work. I will rather be me with my warts and all and not some sleepy, non-feeling zombie. My feelings were and still are trying to tell me something. Sometimes I don't want to listen. I would have stayed stuck in my *Soup* without carefully trusting my own feelings.

I firmly believe that my *Soup* was the direct cause of my depression. I had to be somebody else since being me was wrong during my formative years. Then humiliation and degradation sent me into hiding, not just from others but also from myself. There it is again—that insidious belief that I was somehow born a second-class citizen! There was no room for normal spontaneity in childhood (except for the years with my strange pack of children), or later in life for that matter. I am certain that all of this combined and mixed together is enough to make anybody depressed.

Perhaps it is not so much the actual details, but the confusion, the fogged thinking, and lack of privacy that haunts me. I felt my parent's eyes on me all the time. I had to be "normal" whatever that meant. I couldn't figure out who to be or how to be. I spent all my energy guessing what would give them the least reason to get rid of me. This would be my alter ego for that day. I didn't know as a child that I was hiding or that I changed myself to suit others. It was just happening out of necessity.

To me, depression is about losing oneself, and that is an incredible sad feeling. For years, I didn't know how lost I was, and I didn't know how to begin to find myself or where to look. Depression for me is not to be allowed or welcomed into the world as the person who I am. Depression is to believe all of my parent's lies and internalizing them into my core. Depression is a lot about shame. What if the world could see into me, and find all the dreaded things about me? There must be something fundamentally wrong with me; why else would my parents tell me so. Why else did I have to hide the real me, and be someone else? Depression is shame, and that is a very deeply disturbing feeling. Depression is also a lack of expression, for how can you express yourself, when you don't exist. And no one is listening anyway. For me all the misinformation of the world, my learned chameleon behavior; in short, *The Soup* turned into depression. But I am sure that in other people it can turn into anger or other forms of coping. That depression can physically hurt is not surprising to me. Every cell and nerve are involved. The withheld emotions from years back are like a ticking bomb. The smallest incident can set of the whole avalanche.

Depression can sometimes go so deep that you wonder if the world wouldn't be better off without you. Suicidal thoughts can creep in for many reasons. Sometimes I just wanted peace from my own thoughts, and the worry I had about other people's negative thoughts about me. Other times it was like a final scream for help. A little late, but at least somebody would wonder why she did it. Other times I was just so downright tired that I could hardly put one foot in front of the other. I thought I wasn't worth helping. Or maybe this is how you are supposed to be when you are second-class, and it will never stop. I really didn't think I added anything the world, and the only thing that saved me was the fact I was a mother. I took that responsibility seriously; that meant in those days, that I did my best.

I once read these wise words: "I lived in a glass house into which my mother could look at any time. In a glass house, however, you cannot conceal anything without giving yourself away, except by hiding it underground. And then you can't see it either." I do not know who wrote it, but it is brilliant. A few lines and I could see my situation so clearly.

While living in Denmark, I was mostly friendless and lonely, but I did begin to mingle a little with a couple of women from my son's daycare. I was often too needy and wanted a lot more than they would or could give me. But it was nice to have somebody to talk to at the parent meetings and other events at the daycare. Before this, I had always stood alone. This felt like a small victory and from time to time, when I needed help, they were there for me. I also loved the new feeling I had whenever I met someone at the supermarket and had a small chat. Slowly it merged into a cup of coffee once in a while. Having conversations with other women with small children helped me a lot. I was still shy and second-class and put myself below these women, but it was a beginning.

I knew in my gut that I had to learn to find peace within myself so that I wouldn't need validation from others. I didn't trust myself, and my confidence was under the floorboards. I wanted to talk to people but what could I say and still feel safe at the same time? My thinking was still fogged with rules and crazy ideas of my parents. I was in my early infancy; my learned behavior and unhealthy ways of thinking were beginning to change ever so slightly.

I was beginning to acknowledge my problems and their need for my attention. I had to learn that it was okay to think differently than my mother and that I was not in mortal danger when I disagreed with her. My whole nervous system had always been on high alert since I thought she could control me from afar. It took me a long time to realize that I was letting it happen and that they didn't really have a say anymore. And then it took many more years to realize that I had internalized their "lies." One of them was that I would be found out to be a bad person and send away to die a slow death. It was so insidious, and the fear stayed with me for years; still have it from time-to-time.

The second lie was that I was made to believe that I was a liar and that no one would believe me. For example, one-way it worked was as followed.

One day my mother and I were out shopping, and she ran into an old schoolmate. The woman was very nice and asked me all kind of questions. I answered honestly, but my mother, who obviously didn't want the world to know how we lived at home, smiled at the woman and told her I was such a liar, and that she shouldn't believe anything coming out of my mouth. I was mortified and very ashamed. But if we didn't live the way I saw it, then how did we live? How could I even trust my own truth? And since I had learned that all adults know best, and my mother saw things so differently than I did; it made me the liar. What else could I believe? I still to this day fear that people won't believe me. At the doctor, it is especially bad, and I fear rejection.

I sincerely try to be as honest as possible, and often I am too frank, and hurt people even when that is the last thing I want to do. I know a small white lie can save many situations, but I am fundamentally afraid of being "found out to be a liar." The third lie was that I was second-class. Looking back, it is so sad, and it still haunts me. There are many more layers to the "lies," but I think it is enough for now.

It wasn't an easy task to begin to open my eyes to the fact, that I had not a clue about how to be me, and I had to start sifting through what was the truth and was a misconception. I had no inner compass, but I was eager to learn. My depression began to loosen its grip a little, and now I had a few friends. Slowly, my situation was going in the right direction. As I grew stronger, I also began to see the enormity of my inner turmoil and the sadness over all the wasted time. I saw the years I had spent thinking I was only a puppet in a theater directed by everybody but me, and the years I had only survived but not lived. The saddest thing of all was not being there for my son when he was little and needed me the most. It almost dragged me back into my deep hole of depression. How many more tears and how much more change and growth were needed to find the inner peace that I craved? If I had known, I would have crumbled under the burden. After a couple of months, I began to see my parents again, but I was doing everything possible not to be their little puppet. I didn't want to be back in *The Soup* but, as hard as I tried to stay out of it, my parents tried to get me back in. They didn't like me. As my mother would say, "Where is my happy little girl?" *That's me—the one that wears a mask.* They are my parents, and we will try and work it out, so I began to see them again, and they had missed my son a lot. And he had missed them too.

SNIPPET SIXTEEN:
MEETING MY NEW HUSBAND

My newly found "inner strength" did begin to show in other parts of my life. I didn't stand out as much at work. I began to have some energy to see what was going on around me. I had always looked down to the ground, and I had missed a lot of what was happening around me, including some smiling faces here and there. Maybe the world wasn't interested in hurting me, so I felt a little safer...during the day that is. The night terrors were still there every night. My shy son also opened up, ever so slightly. Of course, bad things happen to everybody and not every day was perfect. It was the first time since leaving my pack of kids in my early teens that I began to feel a sense of belonging in the world. That was huge for me! I had an enormous longing to belong to a group. *Belonging.* I can taste the word in my mouth, the warmth in my stomach. It's the opposite of not fitting in, of being different and "second to everybody else." Hallelujah! Thanks angels. I warned myself—small steps Kirsten. *Don't get overexcited.* I liked the taste. I wanted more.

The saying is that time goes fast when you are having fun. Fortunately, time ran away with me too and, before I knew it, my son was going to preschool. In Denmark, we begin school a little later than here in the US. So, my son was six-years-old and not ready at all. He feared new things and school scared him a lot; I had taught him well. I followed him to school the first week, but after that, he had to go by himself on his bike or on foot. We would leave together in the morning. He went to school, and I walked in the other direction to the train station. I wouldn't be back from work when the school was done, but there was an after-school daycare center close by. I do not believe he liked school one bit, but he loved the after-school program. He was always playing and having fun when I picked him up. For about a year, I had a good job very close to his school and didn't have to take the train into Copenhagen. That was wonderful. We would bike together! We had so much more time together, and life was a lot less stressful. I would venture a small "we were happy, " and I began to have hopes for the future. But one day, I came home, and there was the dreaded letter. *We regret to inform you...* I did fall apart but not as deep as before.

For a short time, I worked for an import/export company. One day the owner needed me to translate for him. He had met a businessman in Wiesbaden, Germany and now this person was coming to Copenhagen. We went to The Sheraton Hotel and picked him up and drove to our office so that business could begin. I didn't know it then, but apparently, Mr. Businessman was more interested in me than in the meeting. About one month later, he called me at the office and invited me out to dinner. He was in transit through Copenhagen and would love to meet with me. I was flattered and thought *why not.* He seemed like a really nice man. This was the beginning of the longest courtship ever. I didn't know it at the time, but he soon told me that he was a married man and that his wife was sick with "alcoholism." He said that he would never be able to leave her but that he would love to have a relationship with me, for as long as I wanted.

At first, I thought that this was crazy. He is asking me to be his mistress! At that, I threw my morals out of the window. He was fun to be with and since he didn't care why should I care. And to hell with what people would think. We genuinely cared for each other. We were like two lonely souls who could help each other. We set off on a very unusual life together and apart. He would come to Copenhagen several times a year, and we would go to lovely restaurants and spend fabulous times together.

His job took him all over the world, so we began to travel together. We zigzagged across every continent and visited many countries. It sounds too good to be true, and sometimes I wondered when it would all end. I lived in my small apartment in Denmark and had this surreal life from time-to-time. I felt like Cinderella...but there was this problem. I lived contradictory lives, and they were just not compatible. I often wondered what if something happened to Nick. I probably would never be told, and I would be back in the ashes. After a while, my son began to travel with us. I loved it but felt I was setting us up for a big, rude awakening one day.

There were days when I was mad inside. Nick was living this wealthy life in Switzerland with another woman, and I could hardly make ends meet back in Denmark. I know I had gone into this relationship with open eyes and we had a ton of fun together. I had never felt so special in all my life. There was never one day in all those years that he didn't call me and it would be hard to give him up. The warning signs were already there and loudly ringing.

One weekend, I was meeting Nick in London while my parents were looking after my son. On my way to the airport, I didn't feel good, but I decided to fly out anyway. I got to London and had to take the underground to the hotel where Nick would meet me. My leg was hurting really bad, and I was feeling very weak. I didn't know that I had a deep vein thrombosis or DVT in my leg. To make a long story short, it moved to my lung that night. I nearly drowned in my own blood. I was taken to the intensive care unit at a hospital near the hotel. It was a real close call, and we were both very scared. I was sicker than a dog and Nick had to go home to his life in Switzerland. Nick had to call my family and inform them that I would not be home for a while because I was in the hospital. After a few days, I was well enough to be taken to a regular medical ward. The doctor told me to quit smoking forever, or it would not have been worthwhile to save me. I never smoked another cigarette.

After about two weeks, I had to go home to Denmark. I was still too sick to go alone and not allowed to travel by air. Nick came to London, and together we took a ferry from England to Denmark. It was nice to be with Nick again and even lovelier to be with my son again. It had been a very traumatic experience for him.

Nick had to go back home, and I was left behind. I was way too sick to look after myself. My girlfriend from the old daycare was absolutely amazing.

She invited my son and me to live with her and her family until I was well enough to look after myself again. She didn't live far away from my home or from school. She made breakfast lunch and dinner for the two of us and took care of me. I knew my son was very mad at me, but I was too sick to deal with it. He coped with the situation but not much more. I was feeling that I was failing him again. We could never have a normal family life as long as I was with Nick and my son craved a stable life. I had a lot of time to think about it all. I can't remember how long we stayed—a month maybe two. I took me a long time to get better, and the Danish hospital was not very helpful. They insisted that I had had a bad case of pneumonia and not a blood clot, as diagnosed by the English doctors. They took me off the blood-thinning medication. You might have guessed already that I was never impressed with the Danish health system.

Our weird life together and apart had now lasted about six years. My son was getting older, and he was getting into trouble at school. He didn't want to do his homework and was very unhappy. It was hard to live this double life, even though it sounds so fabulous. Nick was having the same thoughts in Switzerland. One day he called me to say that he had left his wife and was hoping I would come to live with him. He had moved to his ski apartment in the

French Alps and had sent in the separation papers. Over the Easter holiday, my son and I went to visit and to look at schools. It was a very happy time, but we were all a bit nervous. Nick and I had always traveled together and been on constant holiday, but we had never really lived our lives together. I wanted this life with him so badly, but I was also afraid. It was one thing to be his mistress but another to be his family. *Was I good enough?* The old voices were screaming at me.

My son and I moved to Switzerland in August 1990. He started school the next month. It was clear that we both hoped for a better life.

SNIPPET SEVENTEEN:
MOVING TO SWITZERLAND

Now my "second life" had started. Nick's ex-wife stayed in the house, and he found a super nice apartment for us in a small Swiss village. Everything was so cute and pretty. There were: cows in the fields with their bells ringing; flowers in the streets and on every home; and small water fountains on many street corners. It was so clean and neat. I have never seen so many geraniums in my life. It was peaceful, and everyone was busy keeping up their homes and gardens. We had a ton of things to do to get our new home furnished. Believe it or not, we shopped in Hong Kong and London; again, I felt like Cinderella. We also bought a car for me. It's a good thing that I had obtained a driver's license a couple of years before, even though I didn't own a car and rarely had an opportunity to drive.

My first car ever and brand new! I was so scared driving that thing home. I didn't want Nick to know how nervous I was over a small thing like driving. I was scared...driving in a new car in a new country. I didn't know my way around, and this scared me. *What if I made a dent in the car?* I thought that everything belonged to Nick. On the inside, I was thinking like a child. I was afraid that he would be angry with me and throw me out. It felt just like the fear I had during all my childhood. I had already put Nick up on a pedestal so high that I couldn't reach. We were not equal in my brain. This stupid way of thinking was going to bring me down again and again.

I didn't speak French and couldn't speak to my neighbors. I couldn't ask for directions if I needed them and, as much as I had always loved the sound of the French language, it was a bitch to learn. Sometimes the phone would ring, and there would be a French-speaking person on the line. I could do nothing but hang up. It was tough, but I slowly got the hang of it. I found the supermarket, the hairdressers and doctors. It was hopeless to even try to learn the Swiss opening hours. I would often drive into a parking garage and happily notice that it was easy to find a parking place, only to realize it was Monday morning or some other strange time when the stores were closed.

Slowly, it all became routine, and my son began his new school. It was an international school and had students from everywhere. He had to learn English right away and soon after French was on the schedule. I was so nervous for him. He pretty much only spoke Danish, some English but not much. At home, I had translated back and forth. The first day at school, he met a Thai boy who couldn't speak anything but Thai. The two of them became friends, and together they learned English and one day they could actually speak to each other. It usually took about six months before new kids were enrolled in the regular program. I was so amazed and proud of the progress my son was making. In Denmark, he had been the stupid kid of a single mother and here he was respected, and it was expected of him that he would succeed. It was a very different message than the one I had listened to in Denmark. There the teachers told me that he was a very slow learner and maybe not too bright and they treated him as such.

The contrasts were everywhere, and sometimes it was humorous. In Denmark, I used to bike or take the train to work and do my shopping. Therefore, it was almost funny doing parallel parking up against a chauffeur-driven, Rolls Royce outside the school. Not all the students had that kind of transport, but the first Gulf War was going on, so there were many kids from Kuwait. In general, the students came from wealthy homes or were children of diplomats.

I would come to school to pick up my son in a pair of blue jeans, and most of the other parents were wearing Chanel suits and carrying Gucci handbags. I had a hard time seeing myself in those types of clothes. In general, the Swiss and the foreigners living there were formally and expensively dressed. My inner second-class child was quivering. What if they could see through me? I was afraid that they could see that I had grown up poor. In my mind, it made me less than them.

It wasn't a piece of cake for my son either. He was used to having kids around him and playing with them. Just go outside, and there would be kids in the fields. In Denmark, kids played outside a lot but, in Switzerland, we hardly ever saw a child. I often wondered where they all were. I saw them at school, or all dressed up out shopping with their mothers. The school was 20 miles away, and the students were scattered. After school play was limited and he missed being with friends. There were many times he wanted to go home to Denmark. He had been forced into this new life and hated it for a long time. Ever so slowly, he found a new life there.

I often thanked Nick for the opportunity he gave my son. What a difference the private system had on him! A friend once asked my son, "Where do you think you would be today if you had stayed in the public school in Denmark?" His short answer was,

"In prison." He was about 15-years-old at that time. He told me that in the Danish school, he was so unhappy that in the 3rd or 4th grade he would skip classes. I was shocked; the school had never informed me. I knew he wasn't happy, but in my busy life of working and doing all those practical chores, I had not seen the real warning signs.

In my new life, I didn't have to work and had time to be more involved in his life. I was often at school, speaking to his teachers and keeping an eye on how things were going.

It took a while for his English to be good enough to have a real relationship with Nick. He didn't really like to share me with anybody, and he wasn't used to a male figure in his daily life. It wasn't easy, but with patience and love, it worked. We spent a lot of time in Chamonix in the French Alps, where Nick had his condo. We had a lot of time to bond as a new family. Nick taught him to ski and hike. I didn't like downhill skiing, so the two of them had lots of time together—having fun. They would come home after a day of skiing and tell me about all the daring stuff they had done together. It was very good for him to have a man around to do crazy stuff with and Nick was enjoying it too. Nick had never had children, so he was learning on the job. It was fantastic to see how they became father and son. One day my son said, "You know Mom if you and Nick ever split up, I think I will stay with Nick." I could stop feeling bad about moving a preteen to another country and giving him a new dad. Nick later adopted my son, and their relationship has only grown over the years. They had all the normal father-son stuff that goes on while raising a teenager—a real relationship, not a fairytale.

Nick's divorce seemed to go on forever. Finally, after almost two years, we got married. The ceremony was performed at the local post office. At first, I thought it was really odd and pictured myself surrounded by mail while the postman, with cap in hand, stood on a box performing the wedding ceremony. It wasn't really like that at all. In Switzerland every commune has a "marrying Sam," and in our's, it happened to be the postman. He had a small office upstairs. He wore a suit and tie and in a sense wore many different hats. It was a lovely day. The sun was shining, and we were very happy. We had made it, and we had proven everybody wrong. For years, I had been warned: he is too old for you; you are too different; he will never marry you, and a married man is fooling you. It went on and on like that. So, here we were married and still are married 24 years later.

Then we moved into Nick's house. It was a beautiful house, but it wasn't a move I was looking forward to. He lived there for years with his first wife.

I was afraid of the gossip among the neighbors, and I didn't like the feeling of moving into his old life. I would rather have continued in the apartment or moved to "our house" somewhere. I preferred being near my son's school. I didn't dare mention these thoughts more than a couple of times. It was Nick's money, and he made the decisions. My old pleasing patterns hadn't changed. I didn't know it then and had never heard the word codependency. I wasn't dependent on a drug such as alcohol or morphine but addicted to a need to please and never rocking the boat. *Always be there for others Kirsten and don't stand out or demand anything. Feel the needs of others and deny my own!* I was never allowed to make Nick unhappy or—God forbid—angry. I only dared to stand up and look strong, if I knew 100% that Nick wouldn't mind.

It's hard to explain. It all wears you down...like any other drug. My fear of rejection was greater than anything else. I had this need to please and to be dependent on someone else for my validation. I had no real sense of me, and his opinion of me counted. If he could really see inside me, he would hate and reject me. These were my true beliefs. So, we moved into the house, and it took me many years to make it my home. I didn't allow myself in the living room and was always in the kitchen or upstairs. Don't get me wrong it was a great kitchen, but the fact that I couldn't move into "my own" house wasn't funny at all. It was all in my own mind. When Nick traveled, my night terrors were as big as ever. I never told anybody and certainly didn't tell Nick. *What would he think of me?*

Life went on, and in the winter, we went to Chamonix every weekend and skied nonstop. I became a pretty good Nordic skier and loved my long runs alone in the Alps. It was peaceful and healthy, and I had never been in better shape. In the summer, we hiked for hours. Soon I picked up tennis, and it also came easy for me. I had never climbed, hiked, skied or played tennis until my new life in Switzerland. It was surprisingly easy for me to become a sport woman. All the crazy things I had done as a child had taught my body to be a good athlete. The knowledge had seeped into my cells without me even thinking about it. It was fun to be good at something. From then on, sports became a big part of my life.

When school was out, we all traveled around the world and stayed in lavish hotels. We had the life of dreams, and it was all so wonderful.

There was a big crack in the icing. I had no friends, Nick had no friends, and together we had no friends. Nick knew a ton of people around the world through business but didn't have any friends at home in Switzerland or in France for that matter. There was an odd ski pal or two, but we were basically friendless.

When Nick traveled, I became very lonely. I had noticed that Nick didn't seem to mind that there were no friends around us. He was content, but I was craving people. My French was slow in coming, and it was hard for me to have conversations with my neighbors. I did meet some people via my French class, and I did enjoy our time together. I tried to invite some of them home for dinner, but Nick wasn't always happy about that. It was almost as if he didn't want friends. He just wanted to be with me alone and couldn't understand why that wasn't enough for me. It was nice to be so loved, but at times it was suffocating, and his needs for me were never filled. I was the pleasing machine, and I had to keep giving in to him. Slowly, I built up resentment. *Can't he see that I have had my fill? Can't he see that I am crying on the inside?* On and on it went in my head. I felt he couldn't see or hear me. He had fallen in love with this nice girl, and she was supposed to be a certain way. I was beginning to feel that I couldn't live up to it all his expectations. I was not able to say all that. He had given me so much, and I was forever in debt to him. I often felt like the most ungrateful bitch. Here I was with a life of money and travels and, on the surface, seemingly not a worry in the world. I was slowly getting back into *The Soup*. Anger and sadness built up and never got out, and they became bigger and bigger.

My husband worked very hard. When he was home, we always did what he wanted to do...go to Chamonix. Don't get me wrong. I had finally learned to love skiing and hiking, but I felt I was living his life and not mine. We lived in his house and his apartment. We only spent time on his hobbies. He didn't care for a social life, so we didn't have one. *Why can't I just be happy and content with what he gives me? This life is so much better than what I had, and I do love being with him.* It's just that I would like my ideas and the important parts of me to be in this marriage—as equal partners with some from me and some from him. This was never going to happen. He was very set in his ways, and I often felt it was his way or the highway. Sorry for sounding like a broken record, but I felt so stuck.

I was hoping he could read my mind for I didn't dare say any of this. When I felt hurt or not seen, I would go into the bathroom and cry...just as my mother had done. I was desperate for him to see my tears, but I did everything I could to hide them! What a paradox! I wanted him to know me, but I didn't dare be honest about my feelings. *Does that make me a liar? The Soup* was creeping in.

After a good two years in Switzerland, I was introduced to The International Women's Club of Nyon. This was a turning point for me. The Club had about 300 members and grew slowly each year. It was a very active club and, if I wanted, I had something to do every day. I can't remember how many different activities the Club had, but it was a large number. I became active in the Club and got to know many women from every continent. I managed the Club's treasury for almost three years and also helped to write a cookbook, which raised a lot of money for charity. It was very rewarding to be involved in charity work, and I loved it. Every year we had a big bazaar where members sold their handicrafts. The proceeds would go to many different charities, some local and some abroad. I soon had my own stand and would make things all year around. Now I had something productive to do, just like my friends. I have always loved to sew, bake and knit. In general, I loved to use my hands. I especially loved to make traditional Danish Christmas gnomes, tree ornaments and many other Danish crafts. My stand got bigger and more popular every year.

Around the same time, I also got involved with the Danish church in Geneva and pretty much did the same charity work there. I loved being busy and having new friends. I was happy, and it spilled over into other parts of my life and marriage. But again, I was living two separate lives. One life when Nick was traveling. I would be home alone, scared, not getting any sleep; but, it would be the only time I really had a social life. I craved people like a sponge. The other life was when Nick was home. It was always nice to have him back home. The house was empty without him, and it was exciting to be with him. He loved to stay busy, and we did tons of fun stuff. It was also nice to get some sleep.

I felt my life had to be lived when he wasn't around. This meant that things I liked to do were less important. I didn't have the confidence to stand up for my ideas and myself. We always did what my husband wanted to do, and all he wanted was to be in the condo in the French Alps. So, we went there every single weekend. He didn't need any other adults around but me. He was content with his life. I, on the other hand, wanted to have a social life in Geneva. Dinners and other events were always held on the weekends, and we could never go. I tried to suggest that we could stay home, but he wouldn't hear of it. We went to Chamonix. End of discussion. *As if there was ever a discussion in the first place!* I felt like a child who had to do what her parents wanted her to do. We would go to Chamonix, and I would be fuming and crying on the inside…hating myself. *Why am I not allowed to grow up and have my own wants?* My husband had no clue about my inner sadness.

I am beginning to sound like a spoiled child who wants everything her way all the time. That is not what I am trying to say. *The Soup* was getting in the way of my thinking. I never knew that my no really meant no. Looking back at it today, it saddens me that I never did stand up for myself. If I didn't want to go to Chamonix, then don't go, and if he gets pissed off so be it. But the fact that I couldn't do that made the dysfunction grow out of proportion. If I didn't have the right to say no, how could I gladly say yes to anything; things were decided for me. I hated it because it made me feel that I was a child and my husband was my father. And at times I feared him as much; this is not good for the marriage. I have to say, that my husband has never laid a hand on me, never yelled at me and he is a very nice man, but with his control patterns and my pleasing addictions we surely were meant for each other. There was stuff to be learned, we just had not gotten started yet.

I knew somewhere inside me that a lot of my problems had their roots in my childhood and I wanted the problems solved. I began to go see different kinds of doctors and healers. I would do anything, except what it took to grow up and be myself. One particular healer stands out. She lived in a small fishing village on Lake Geneva. She was well known, and people stood in line outside her modest home. Even hospitals called upon her. Switzerland is a lot less concerned with mixing regular medicine with the alternatives methods. She never charged you anything, but she had a little box on her wall. If you felt like giving her money for her services, you could. I visited her a few times. She was a big woman, not given to smiling. She conducted her business in a brusque fashion. You had to go through her small kitchen—with her food cooking—and then her living room to get to her little parlor. She had a massage table, a chair, one small alter and nothing else. We never talked much; she just wanted to know what I needed.

It was always the same. I wanted the night terrors to go away, and I wanted to be happy like other people. She would lay me on the table, put a cross on my heart and then she would pray so fast in a language I didn't understand. I would feel very odd and always ended up with hysterical crying. The whole thing lasted about 15 minutes. After the session, she would look at me without a smile and say, "You need to forgive your parents. I want you to go into the church across the street and stay there till it is done. You also need to have your thyroid checked, it's not working well." She was right about the thyroid, but I wasn't ready to forgive my parents, even if it could help me get some sleep. I had so much pent up anger inside me. Why on earth should I forgive them? They had treated me badly, and I was the victim. It never occurred to me then, that with that kind of thinking, I would stay a victim and that somehow, I couldn't grow up and get better.

Is it possible that *The Soup* and the victim feeling something to do with each other? When you are a victim, you are small and insignificant. And by living like that, I didn't have to take responsibility for anything; it would always be somebody else's fault. Just like my mother, I had become a victim, and I knew how to play that role well. My parents were still controlling me.

l looked for something outside of me to cure me...doctors, healers, better friends or a more understanding husband. *Could I do something else?* This question didn't enter my brain. I thought I was at the mercy of whatever came my way. I could still only react and not direct my own life. It felt like being on rocky ground all the time. Whenever the world threw me a curve ball, I would fall apart—every time. I believed I had done something wrong and I was somehow being punished for it.

Life still goes on and has to be lived—whether it functions well or not at all.

SNIPPET EIGHTEEN:
CHANGE OF LIFESTYLE

My son was doing great. He was working hard at school, and his grades were showing it. He had also become an excellent skier and liked our time together in Chamonix. We would sometimes bring a friend of his from school. The boys would have fun skiing and, in the evenings, we would all play games. After a long day of skiing, they practically ate us out of house and home. I have always liked to cook, and a good appetite was welcomed in my house.

Nick and I both wanted our son to get the best education, and we were on the right track. My son was learning from his regular school programs as well as our travels. He could see how people lived all around the world. He was seeing so much and trying so many new things all the time. In the beginning, my son didn't like all the weird foreign food. Soon enough, he would eat whatever he could. Sometimes it was better not to ask what the food was that he was eating. He just ate it.

He was only 12-years-old when we did seven days of white water rafting down the Grand Canyon. It was very exciting but a bit more than I was used to doing. My son did great, but I broke a toe. I get hurt every time that I do things a bit beyond my capabilities. It wasn't a big deal, but it hurt a lot on the long hike out of the canyon. It was a ten-mile hike and gained one mile in elevation. It was a hot day, and we all had a tough time staying hydrated.

We took many trips and visited Asia so often that Malaysia became like a second home. We visited Hong Kong, Singapore, Thailand, Indonesia, China and many major cities in Europe and United States. One time we were flying from San Francisco to Singapore on Christmas Day. My son was mad as hell! How could we do this to him on Christmas? He did have a fun time. There weren't many passengers on the flight, and the stewardesses had nothing to do. They all played Monopoly with him, and that's not something you see every day. Since it's my birthday on Christmas Day, Nick arranged to have a birthday cake for me on the same flight. The crew came and sang Happy Birthday to me in Chinese. It was fun times.

Over the years, we would walk on the Great Wall of China, visit the Xian Warriors, and spend New Year's Eve in Bangkok and much more. My son's teenage years could not have been further away from our poor life of his early years.

Nick was also a demanding dad. No slacking on the hikes. If you want to ski with the big boys, then pull yourself together. Schoolwork and grades were important; morals and work ethics were pounded into him. No sitting around during the summer holidays. When he was only 16, we send him to work in Chicago. He had to get a driver's license in a hurry. In Europe, you can't drive before age 18. He was going to stay and work with a friend and colleague of my husband. After three days, the friend had a death in the family and had to leave the country. My son then stayed alone and drove to work every day in Chicago traffic. I was so scared for him. Our little village near Geneva had only 400 people, and the American traffic scared me. I told him he could come home at any time if he wanted. He stayed in Chicago and learned a lot about his own strengths.

The next year we sent him to work at an oil factory in mainland Denmark—not too close to my family. He lived in a school dorm and met a ton of fun people. He again learned to take care of himself. He was never allowed to just sit around and do nothing for the summer, except for the last summer before going off to college. We went on safari in several African countries. It was a new and fantastic experience and also a learning one. The Africans are poor. It was an eye opener for him to see a woman washing her clothes in a pothole in the road. Life is hard in Africa. We had also seen poverty in Asia. In Africa, it was more in your face, and you never felt safe in the big cities.

My son also learned not to take money for granted. You work hard for what you have. You spend wisely and always save for a rainy day. You don't think that you are better than others just because you have more money. Don't ever look down at people who are struggling.

Then one day the nest was empty. We all flew to New York and drove up to Troy, NY. He went to his new school and home and stayed for the next four years. Nick and I both had backaches from stress, but our son was upbeat and said. "Nick, you just adopted me. I am a Gershon now, and The Gershons always make it." And he was so right. He went through college with flying colors. I was so proud of him. Not bad for a kid who the Danish school system had given up on in first grade.

The Danes always talk about our wonderful egalitarian society, but I guess some are more equal than others. I always felt that it was easy to say to a single mother that her son was a bit stupid. I do not think that they would have said the same thing to a married couple with good educations. It is always easy to kick somebody who is already down. So much for social justice, understanding and support of the less fortunate in society. It may make me sound a bit bitter, and you may think that I exaggerate. I have tried to live both lives...the poor and the rich. I can attest to the fact that wherever you are in the world, you are treated with a lot more respect and kindness if you have money. It's a sad fact but nevertheless a fact.

OPENING UP TO SECRETS

I began therapy around the time my son left for college. I felt so empty and thought it might help to talk to somebody. At that time, I was still pretty unaware of the depth of my wounds and my unhealthy thinking. All I knew was that no matter where I lived or with whom I lived, I didn't know how to fit in or what to do to be an equal partner. I always knew that there was more to my problems than the feeling of not fitting in. I found myself a therapist and began to work. I went to Madame Fleur for a while, and she helped me with my fogged thinking and misinterpretations of the world. She slowly helped me change my mental programming. Her best advice was: the best way to look after others is to look after

yourself. Earlier I would have equated that with egotism. I soon noticed a change in the people around
me. When I began to take care of myself, they didn't
have to worry about me. Therefore, they could take
care of themselves.

After some time, I felt that I had to see a therapist who spoke Danish and who was used to dealing
with sexual abuse. This was very important to me,
even though I had never really mentioned that side
of my problem. I was way too ashamed and confused
and didn't know how to address the issue. I knew it
had to be done in my own language.

So, I found a woman in Denmark who was willing
to work with me…one hard, emotionally draining
week after another. I would fly up from Switzerland
to Copenhagen and work two hours a day for a
week. Then I flew home. I was a wreck! Back in
Switzerland, I would phone her a bit and then, some
months later, fly back up for another week. It was
not an easy process, but I am so glad I did it. I usually stayed with a friend and thanked God for that.
There were days when I felt like falling apart. It was
hard, and I felt like I was splitting in two. The denial
and the voices inside of me were at war. *I can't believe
I am writing it down.* In therapy, I would talk about it
and then three seconds later I would deny it. It is so
deeply hidden inside me that I couldn't really look
at it. I also knew that if I didn't, I would never get

well. So, here it is. I believe I was sexually abused as a child.

It's not like I was attacked and raped by family members. It was more the fact that my body didn't belong to me. I was used for the benefit of my mother, just as I was used on an emotional level. My thoughts on this subject were still fogged, and my inner children were very scared.

I can't initiate sex. If I do, then I am dirty, and it shows that I might enjoy sex. If you like sex, you are a dirty little bitch. I am somehow not a normal human being with normal sexual feelings and reactions, but a dirty bitch. Who taught me that? I have late in life learned about carried shame, which means that the abuser goes free and the victim carries all the bad feelings especially the shame. The abuser feels no guilt, but the victim/child believes that they are bad and filthy. All children need affection, but they should not be used to take care of adults needs.

My parents lived in an emotionally cold and un-rewarding marriage. My dad was the boss, and there was no equality in their "partnership." He would humiliate and degrade my mother and she never ever stood up for herself. I never once saw them hug each other or show any form of affection. It was cold between them. I can't to this day understand how they managed to have four children. My father loved his own tyranny and sarcasm. It never entered his brain that he was ruining everything for us all, including for himself.

My father was thrown out of his home as a pre-teen. I believe that he never developed into a responsible adult. He never washed much, and he would wear the same shirt for days on end, even sleeping in it. I always felt a mixture of disgust and fear around him. But did he actually sexually abuse me? I don't think so. I often wonder why I am so scared of a man entering my bedroom every single night of my life. I do remember as a young teenager he would comment on my developing body, and I hated it. I was always afraid of him seeing me nude. I would always hide. I would bring all my clothes with me into our tiny little bathroom. I would rather wear wet clothes than to have him see any part of me. No locks or keys were allowed in our household, not even for the bathroom. The fear of someone walking in unexpectedly was huge. So, my showers were very quick and not enjoyed. I can still remember hurriedly putting on my underwear while I was still damp and, at the same time, trying to hold the door closed.

I have always felt my father's eyes on me—whether he was actually seeing me or not—smirking. I felt like my body was to be ridiculed like the rest of me. My father would comment on my new small breasts and loved to see me squirm. It didn't feel safe being a woman and I had learned early on that men were in charge and more powerful than women. I was very ashamed of my new changing body, and I hated to grow up to be a woman.

Sex was never ever mentioned in my childhood home. All bodily functions were embarrassing and not to be talked about at all. I felt that my mother had two sides to her. She was a prudent, subservient and a depressed victim. Sex is only for dirty girls and whores. She was the victim, and she used it. In her victimhood, she was never responsible for anything. She was so anti-sex that sexual organs weren't to be mentioned. She couldn't even tell her daughters about menstruation and other women's issues. Sexuality is best kept a secret. The other side of my mother was craving affection. She was starved for love and probably sex as well and, if you can't get it from your husband, you can take it from your children. I wasn't very old when I realized that my mother's hugs and kisses were meant for someone else. It always felt dirty, and I tried to avoid her. I have many memories of my mother getting her adult needs met by me.

For a very long time, my mother slept on a sleeper sofa with me. I was the little child and loved having mother next to me. She loved me so much she would rather sleep with me than with dad. Her neediness, her strong smells and her touch still made me sick. She took what she needed, and her little daughter didn't know any better. She thought she was a good little girl, making mother happy. During the day, anything sexual or affectionate was seen as wrong and dirty—at night it was different. I began having nightmares of being killed and of being smothered to death. My mother was a very big woman, and I often felt overwhelmed. The fear of being sent away was always with me. I began to wonder where my sister slept. We used to share the bedroom. *Why can't we always sleep in the same beds like other people did?* It was so confusing to me. And it certainly wasn't anything I could talk about. I knew that this was not to be talked about—ever.

As I grew older, mother and I stopped sleeping in the same bed, and my sister and I were back in the same sleeper sofa. I actually never had my own bed. It wasn't easy for two sisters to sleep together like that. But that was life in our small apartment. We didn't really get along, and I often wished I could have my own bed or better my own room. I don't remember how old I was, but I had mixed feelings about my mother. All children want attention, and I do remember missing my mother, but I also remember the relief it was to not be with her. My feelings were very confused. I was old enough to know that other children did not sleep with their parents. My relationship with my mother became unbearable. I loved her. I wanted to help her, solve all her problems, make her happy and I hated her. Sometimes I was so angry and confused I just wanted to scream. But, like the good little girl I was, I never said anything. *Keep it in and pretend life is good.*

Bodily functions were also taboo during my childhood, but my mother developed this need to have me with her in the bathroom. She wanted me there when she was doing her business. I do not know if it was a form of exhibitionism or it was a way to deal with the forbidden. She would also walk in on me even when I was an adult. She would be talking and pretending it was normal. I hated being there with her. I felt like I was dirty and used.

I hate bathrooms, and I don't like to shower in public. Since sports activities have become an important part of my life, I am often in public bathrooms. I always find a corner where I can be by myself, as private as possible. When people speak to me through a closed toilet door, I get angry and feel invaded. As I grew older, I learned not to be available to mother, but she would find ways to lure me into the bathroom. She would invent cancerous lumps in her groin. "I think I have cancer. Could you feel here?" She would still try when I was an adult married woman. There are other memories, but I have to wait with sharing them till I get stronger.

AWFUL WOMANHOOD

Another area where my mother was extremely invasive was in my development into a woman. I had never in my life heard of menstruation and one day I was bleeding. I thought I was sick. During my childhood, I had one urinary tract infection after the other, and I thought it was getting really bad. My stomach was hurting, and I didn't feel good. I had to go to my mother. She explained to me that all women had to endure "the red shit" every month. Males were never to be told, and the smell and the embarrassment had to be kept a secret. She gave me some horribly old-fashioned pads to wear. I cried and hated to be a woman. She never told me it had to do with being able to bear children or anything positive. Being a woman was a bitch! Every month it came back with terrible cramps and fainting spells.

I often felt so bad that I couldn't go to school for a day or two.

My mother pretended to care, but she was getting some kind of pleasure from checking my pads and talking about how much blood I was losing. She would come right into the bathroom while I was sitting there. The room would be spinning, and I was half-fainting. She demanded to see the pad. My huge mother would tower over me and not give me one inch of privacy. *Does she think she is a good mother? I hate her. I need her.* I was stuck as usual. There was nowhere to go for safety. I hated the whole damn thing and the thought that I was going to have "the red shit" all my life was depressing.

I remember seeing the family doctor for the painful cramps and fainting. I told him the pain came every time I had "the red shit." He got angry with me and demanded that I call it by its name. I should stop being such a brat for calling it "the red shit." I had only one other word for it: visitors from Russia. This was another term my mother would use. I thought that I better not try that. But since I was there, he decided to give me a gynecological exam. I was about 12 or 13 and all of a sudden I found myself in a horrible situation. My old, male doctor tells me how to lie down the right way. No gowns like today and no privacy for undressing. Spread your legs and let me do the examination. I had no idea what was coming.

No explanation or comforting words beforehand. No one is telling me what was going to happen or why it was happening. I didn't know what the hell he was doing. I wanted to scream and couldn't relax. I was in shock and felt raped. He had probably done this kind of exam on many adult women, but I was a child. I had never had intercourse, and I had no idea about how I functioned down there. The whole female anatomy was dirty to me. And now this man was seeing and touching this disgusting part of me. No words can describe how I felt at that moment. There was no adult consent; my mother wasn't with me. She had not been with me to the doctors for a long time. This was another thing to do alone. I was alone with this man, and I didn't know what to do. He had already scolded me for "the red shit," so I didn't want to make him angry with me again. I had no clue that I could have resisted or even said no.

After the exam, he washed his hands and told me everything seemed normal. He acted like nothing had happened. I could hardly stand. I don't remember saying anything, and somehow, I got myself dressed and walked out of there. One more thing you have to endure as a woman. Why were people so interested in sex? I found the whole thing revolting. I swore I would never have anything to do with it. I felt degraded and humiliated and yes—in a sense—I was raped. It would have been nice to have a woman there with me but not my mother. I had the same doctor for many more years. In Denmark, it isn't easy to change your family doctor and certainly not when you are just a child. I never told my mother or anyone. How could I tell? I didn't have the right words, and she was already way too interested in me as it was. Here was yet another thing to file under confusing "terrible woman stuff."

I left humiliated, red-faced and scolded. My self-esteem was under the floorboards again. Slowly, the other girls at school began to get their periods, and they talked about it. They obviously knew all the right words and didn't have to wear old-fashioned pads. How embarrassing! I didn't ever talk to my sister about it. It had to be kept so secret. Some years later, I do remember being surprised finding pads in my sister's drawer. Somehow it had never occurred to me that she too would have the "red shit."

I really wished that I had had a grown woman to talk to or to guide me. This new world of becoming a woman was getting very scary. I hated my body, and I hated the confusion. Somehow, I was supposed to know it all and gracefully change into a swan. Well, that didn't happen, and for many years, I stayed a small girl inside a woman's body.

One incident did help me understand a few things. Shortly after moving away from home with my boyfriend at the age of 18, I woke up with a huge pain in my stomach. It became so bad that we had to call 911 and I was rushed to the hospital. About three months prior, I had seen my infamous doctor because something wasn't right with my female parts. He gave me a referral to see a specialist. The waiting list was long and, while waiting, I ended up in the emergency room. First, one doctor came in and examined me and then another. Finally, Mr. Big Shot doctor came with his trail of many students. All this time, which seemed like hours, I was in the most dreaded and defenseless position for a woman. I was never asked if it was okay having all these people looking right up my most private and shameful parts. I was a very shy, 18-year-old and, in that moment, in a lot of pain. All these people, who were not much older than I was, were discussing my female parts like I was a piece of meat. It was so embarrassing. I wished that God would open up the floor so I could sink away. No one spoke to me. After they had left, I was sobbing in shame. Then, after an eternity, I was told that I had a cyst on an ovary and that it had exploded. This was why I had the pain. I needed surgery right away. The whole ordeal was awful, but I met some real women, and that was worth it.

I was in a ward with about six women who had all been through gynecological surgery of some kind. We were between the ages of 18 and 45. These women were so wonderful. I was almost sad going home. I had never met women who were proud to be women and who talked naturally about their sexuality. Nothing was off the table. At first, I was mortified. Slowly, I began to notice that I was learning a lot from the experiences that these women shared. They were not hiding themselves and didn't feel less-than-others just because they were women. They were not scared or ashamed of their own sexuality. I began to think a little differently about the whole woman thing—maybe I had misunderstood something important. No one had ever told me that being a woman made me special. We are here to bear children and love them. Of course, I knew about the birds and the bees (known in Denmark as the "flowers and bees"). I had never looked at it as anything special, just another way to hurt us. Women can be the most loving and giving creatures. Being a woman is a gift, not a curse. I knew I had to go home and chew on that one for a while. Surgery wasn't fun, but I would not have liked to be without that learning week with real, everyday women.

MORE SECRETS

My mother's half-brother Alfred was a problem in my childhood. He and his wife often came to visit. I do not know what his problem was, but he was always talking about sex. It was never in a direct way. He always told very dirty stories and jokes and didn't care if the children were there. When we became teenagers, he loved to tell stories about having sex with farm animals. It made me sick to my stomach. I never understood why my parents would listen to this stuff. His wife always referred to him as an old pig. His adult daughter refused to be around him and disallowed him entrance to her home. He always gave us money for ice cream or sweets. He especially liked my older brother.

As I grew older, I hated his persona, and I would do anything to not be near him and not hear his jokes. He always came across as such a nice friendly man, but I thought he was slimy. His stories were the worst stories, and my uncle loved to tell them over and over again. They haunted me for years and overwhelmed my childhood brain. I don't know if they were real stories or fantasies. It didn't really matter. Either way, it was more than I could cope with as a child or as an adult for that matter.

He would begin the story with stupid little anecdotes about sex, and then his stories would evolve into more wild terrain. His story would go to a barnyard where he was having sex with sheep. He would put the two hind legs into his rubber boots and, as the poor animal was trapped, he would proceed to do his ugly business. At the end of his story, he would be standing and do lovemaking movement with his body and his face would be lit up and happy. His wife would try to stop him but always failed. My mother who had grown up with him didn't know what to do. She ended up laughing with him, and my dad thought it was really funny.

No one seemed to mind about the small children who were listening. I always felt dirty after those stories. I instinctively knew they were bad and shouldn't have been told at all. To me, adults were horrible people—period. I do believe that my Uncle Alfred, who was a lot older than my mother, was a big reason for my mother's problems. I can't know that as a fact, but once, when I was visiting my mother, she was complaining that Uncle Alfred's daughter didn't want him in her life. My mother felt sorry for him and went on and on about my poor uncle being snubbed by his own daughter. I finally said, "Maybe there is a good reason for her not wanting him in her life." I had hardly finished the sentence when my mother turned around and faced me in anger and uttered, "and that shall never be talked about." She was so forceful in her reaction towards me that I have always had an inkling that I was on to something. In a sense, she validated my thoughts.

I do remember him at my confirmation. We were having a small party, and after lunch, he wanted to dance with me. I wanted the floor to swallow me, and I told my mother that I didn't want to dance with him. She literally forced me to dance. She said, "It's your day, and you get to dance with every person at the party." She didn't see the plea in my eyes, or maybe she was so used to him that his behaviors had become normal to her. Danced we did. He was pushing me hard into his erection all the time. I was mortified and wanted to die on the spot. He had a wonderful time while he ruined my day.

Mentioning my confirmation, I better tell the rest of the story. In Denmark, everyone is Lutheran. We have state churches, pay church tax, and the schools are involved in the teaching of religion. You are allowed to opt-out if you were a non-believer or from a different religion. When I was a kid, I would say that 99% had the same faith. Usually, around 13-or 14-years-old, the whole school grade began to prepare for confirmation. I remember going to the pastor to take lessons, but I wasn't impressed. I hardly understood a word he said. He wasn't very good at explaining anything, and I hadn't found a real reason to believe in God. The God he talked about wasn't as sweet as my angels, but I listened and maybe learned a thing or two. Eventually, the big day arrived. For me, confirmation was about being the right thing to do. Everybody else was being confirmed, and it was part of growing up as a Danish kid.

My parents had no money and confirmations were expensive. The party and the new clothes were a lot for them. Since my brother was only one year older than I was, they told him to wait a year and to be confirmed on the same day as me, not together with his schoolmates. Poor him! He was not allowed to have his own day and had to be with his younger sister and her peers. It was pretty embarrassing for him. I felt so sorry for him that I almost forgot that I didn't have my own day either.

Confirmation brings up some guilty feelings inside me. They have been with me forever and, in this moment, I feel as if it all happened yesterday. I was going shopping for confirmation clothes with my parents. First, they bought me a white dress for the actual confirmation. Then, as the best Danish tradition demanded, my parents had to buy me second-day clothes...something nice for the next day. The white dress was easy, but the other set of clothes was not. My parents were going to spend money on me, and I felt so special. We went to a real clothes shop, not to the cheap warehouses we would normally go. I had mainly worn hand-me-downs and whatever my mother bought for me.

Now, I was inside this beautiful boutique. I didn't even know such stores existed. The three of us must have looked a little out of place, and I can still remember the feeling of inadequacy. I wanted to be like the other customers, sophisticated and smart. I was to have a dress, shoes and a coat. I had absolutely no idea what I liked—what was fashion or what it could cost. All I could think in my panic was, "What the girls at school would think?" What do my parents want me to have?" The prices were scaring me. I swear I didn't know what to do and felt like the most ungrateful girl in the world. My parents wanted to please me, but I was paralyzed and couldn't think. I followed my father's eyes and bought what he wanted and not what I wanted. My pleasing instinct had never been on higher alert. I ended up with a dress I only wore once, a pair of boots that the girls laughed at and a salmon-colored coat that was way too adult for a young teenager. I never wore the coat. My parents kept asking about it. I didn't and couldn't tell them the truth. I was so ashamed, and to this day I want to cry over the whole affair. Every day that I opened my very Spartan wardrobe, those three items haunted me. *Your parents buy you real clothes. They spend a lot of money on you. You don't wear them. You are an ungrateful failure of a person.*

The fear of ridicule at school was greater than my parent's begging eyes. It was the first time in my life I was going to be spoiled a little, and I ruined it for everybody. I have never really overcome the feeling of letting my parents down. I really wanted blue jeans. Everybody was wearing blue jeans. I wasn't allowed to have blue jeans. They were out of reach for me. At her confirmation the next year, my sister got blue jeans and a blue jeans jacket. I was so envious, sad and angry. I convinced myself that I hated blue jeans and didn't own a pair until my life in Switzerland many years later. I even believed my own story until my husband asked me, "Why don't you ever wear blue jeans?" It had been easier for me to hate the jeans than to deal with the sadness.

So...finally the confirmation day arrived, and my parents had invited uncles, aunts and grandparents from my father's side of the family. (My mother's parents had passed a long time ago.) These were people

I hardly knew. There were about 24 to 28 people, and we all had to fit into our little apartment. The day before the big event, we moved furniture around, emptied the living room and filled it up again with rented tables and chairs. It was very cramped but pretty with white starched tablecloths and napkins. Flowers were bought too. It certainly didn't look like our living room anymore. My mother had hired a cook to help her with the meal. I was very excited but my brother less so, for obvious reasons. I had a new, long, white dress and I felt like a million dollars. I recently saw pictures from the confirmation. My brother and I look unhealthy and overweight from eating the wrong foods. We were well dressed, and we were ready. My mother had one panic attack after another and I do not think she enjoyed any of it.

The confirmation was held in the morning. We all went to church as a family, which was not something we did very often. I was a bit scared about it all, but it all went well, and soon we were all back in the apartment. We sat down for a typical Danish meal: soup, roast and ice cream. Family members had created songs—songs about my brother and me. They were a lot of fun. There were lots of speeches. The whole thing was very formal, but also festive. The uncles began to get a little drunk, not to mention my father's stepmother—the woman who had thrown him out of his childhood home so many years ago. I couldn't stand her, but somehow, she had the honor of being my Godmother. She was never in my life, and I never heard from her after my confirmation.

After the lunch tables and chairs had been removed, there was some room to dance. My family had never had a party before, and dancing was certainly not an event I was used to seeing. I was enjoying it all until the dance with Uncle Alfred. After the dance with my uncle, I stopped being part of it all and disappeared inside myself. The only memories that I have after that moment are cleaning up and moving the furniture back the next day.

As I look back at my confirmation and my childhood as a whole, I firmly believe that I was sexually abused as well as neglected as a child and that caused me to believe that I was a nasty person. It made me ugly and unworthy. Over the years, I used enormous energy to push all this away from me. I tried to deny it, tried to tell myself I am making it all up and tried to normalize it. I have wanted to end it all—anything to never confront or even feel the emotions that belong to that sad part of me. I always knew that I had to hide it all from the world. It was my secret and, if I ever told, no one would believe me or even worse, I would be hated and loathed. No one would want to be near me—this piece of filth. I hid it well. For many years, I didn't think about it. It had altered my personality, and I always felt that the world was an unsafe place. I also knew that these secrets made me unlovable and used—like old clothes. When all this was added to my already shattered self, you found a scared, confused, and very sad girl and later a very sad woman.

I have only recently allowed myself to talk about this. I still worry about what people might think, but I worry most about what my siblings will think about me. I have come to the conclusion that this is my life. This is my truth and whether it happened to them or not is not important. What is important is that I finally found my own voice. I can say that terrible, ugly things were done to me and it wasn't my fault. I didn't want it, and I am not to be blamed. If somebody should carry the burden, it should be the perpetrators and not me.

This is a very new way of thinking, but I love it. It sets me free. I was used and abused, but it doesn't make me a bad person. Hallelujah!

SNIPPET TWENTY-TWO:
AMERICA

S ome years after my son moved to the United States to study and my husband had retired, I began to talk about living somewhere new. At first, my husband didn't even want to hear about it. My husband loved to be in Switzerland and liked that we could be in a different country in a few hours or less. He loved going for long weekends to little towns with great restaurants. He loved the change of atmosphere that you can get from country to country and from town to town. I didn't feel that I fit in and I wanted a change. Since my husband is 23 years older than I am, I preferred to start a new life before he would be too old to move. I dreaded to think about living in Switzerland alone as I aged. Who knows? He is in a lot better health than I am and maybe he will outlive me.

My husband wanted to go to Italy or Spain. I thought it wouldn't be any different from Switzerland. The thought of learning yet another language didn't appeal to me. I wanted to go to the United States of America. After a long period of discussions, we decided to try it out. In 2007, we moved to Albuquerque, New Mexico. We wanted a place with sunshine, skiing and lots of tennis. We also wanted a good size town but not so big that traffic would be a problem. We went to New Mexico a couple of times and loved it there. We bought a house and thought we would live in New Mexico in the winter and in Switzerland in the summer. After just one winter in Albuquerque, we were in love with the American way of living, the positive outlook and the smiles. I have never met nicer people than the folks in Albuquerque. We were welcomed into people's lives and homes. Everybody was so helpful and making friends was super easy. In addition, there is a lot more for seniors to do in the US than in any country in Europe. We joined a fitness/tennis club and practically lived there. In Switzerland, you do not see many seniors. Just like the children, they just are not around. I had never seen groups of 70-year-olds play tennis before living in the US. It was an inspiration, and the thought of growing old in that atmosphere was very appealing. We went back to Europe and sold everything and have never looked back—well, except for the European food and cute little towns.

We didn't live there long before we had many friends. Soon I was on a fun and competitive tennis team. We played a lot and sometimes even traveled to other states to play. They were great girls. There was a different freedom in America that I had ever known. Just be yourself, and that will be enough. What a concept. I didn't feel judged. For the first time in my life, I felt that I fit in. It was a feeling I had longed for and never thought I would find. Albuquerque had become home. I loved being in America, and I didn't have to work at fitting in; it just happened

Since I had so enjoyed working with a charity in Switzerland, I began to wonder if I could do something in Albuquerque. I decided to make custom earrings, a few necklaces and, of course, my Danish gnomes. It was hard at first and tough to find venues. After a while, people began to invite me to tennis tournaments and into businesses. I had many open houses. All proceeds went to charity. I didn't take a penny towards materials or my time. It was fun when people began to know me. They heard my name and said, "You are the earring lady." Most of the money collected I gave to a preschool in a poor neighborhood. The rest I gave to cancer research. It was a great way to get to know people and, at the same time, do some good for the poor in town.

We loved Albuquerque and thought we were going to live there for the rest of our lives. Sadly it was not to be.

My body began to fall apart. I had thyroid problems, and then I developed some weird pneumonia and had to take antibiotics for more than three years. The disease didn't seem to go away. I didn't really feel sick, but I was tired a lot and sensed that something was wrong. After three years, I had had enough. I was beginning to think that the pills would kill me before the disease. I decided to go to the famous National Jewish Hospital in Denver, Colorado. They gave me a ton of expensive tests and declared that I didn't have pneumonia. I had acid reflux, and the acid was hurting my throat and my lungs. A whole week of tests and all they could come up with was acid reflux. So, they gave me two different kinds of acid reflux pills. The instructions were, "Take them for the rest of your life." Really, I thought? They also told me to get rid of the antibiotics, but my doctor in Albuquerque disagreed with them.

My infection was still somewhere in my body, and my Albuquerque doctor wanted to give me even more antibiotics, maybe another year or two. I refused. Then he gave me statins for elevated cholesterol. "Take them for the rest of your life," he said. *Too many pills.* I felt I was eating handfuls of pills. In Europe, I had taken an odd pill here and there for a headache or after my blood clot but never for the rest of my life. I decided to throw away the statins, the antibiotics and finally the acid reflux medications. I had never felt any acid reflux before but now my stomach was so used to the medication, it didn't know how to regulate itself anymore. I persevered with diet and patience. I am not saying that everybody should throw their medications away like I did. I am just telling my story.

I was not getting better. I became sicker and sicker, and no one could tell me what it was. Living at high altitude (6,200 feet) didn't help. It added to the stress on my body. I had noticed that I felt a lot better whenever I was at a lower altitude. Slowly, I began to lose my memory and worried that I might have Alzheimer's disease. I was so tired all the time and, for the first time in my life, I slept like a baby. It was not normal to sleep more than 16 to 18 hours a day. I couldn't function. My husband and I began to get really worried—only 55-years-old and sick as a dog. What was going on?

I had taken myself off the antibiotic and began to think that I made a mistake. I got so bad that I couldn't drive a car, couldn't play tennis and couldn't think straight. My vision was changing, and I had constant headaches. I couldn't hydrate no matter how much I drank. We began to think about moving to a lower altitude. I was not happy, and I didn't want to move, but we couldn't see any other solution.

At about the same time, we were considering buying a new home in Tucson, Arizona, I was diagnosed with Addison's disease. I was in my doctor's office and totally dehydrated. I had given up and had resigned.

Thank God my husband was with me. I wouldn't have remembered anything. My doctor asked me to count backwards, but I couldn't; my brain wouldn't function. He spoke to my husband about sending me to a hospital, but suddenly he said, "I am sure she has Addison's disease. We can spend a week testing her, but she doesn't have a week before she will die from dehydration and volume depletion. Let's just give her the medication and see what happens."

I had never heard of Addison's disease. It had taken a good year or more to get that diagnosis. When I took my first hydrocortisone pill, it was awesome. It was like watering an old dried out plant and seeing it come back to life. It was so amazing, but now I was back on more pills. Steroids for life. I didn't want the damn pills, but without them, I would wither away and die. In the back of my head, there is little nagging thought. *Do I have Addison's disease or do I have something else that reacted well on the same medication?* I went to a specialist in endocrine diseases, and he was not helpful. I left with more questions! I was so underwhelmed by him that I asked him if he actually had the nerve to send me a bill. He did. I didn't think he deserved a penny, but the good girl paid anyway.

We decided to go ahead with the move to Tucson. I read a lot about Addison's disease and realized that it had a lot to do with stress. Addison's is a disease of the adrenal gland. The adrenal gland is responsible for dealing with stress, hydration, and a ton of other functions. It's pretty important, and you can't live without it. So here I am thinking—no wonder my adrenal gland conked out on me. It would be hard to find anybody who had been more stressed than I was.

I hated taking all that medication and tried whatever it took to get off of them.

It is amazing how the established doctors and the alternative practitioners differed in their understanding of the world and the treatment of diseases. I wish that the line between them could be more blurred and that the two sides could learn to work together. At the moment, I am treating my Addison's disease with hydrocortisone, and that is for life. *Don't you dare get off it because you may die.* The alternative practitioners told me that it was possible for the body to heal itself. I do not know if I believe them, but I am willing to try anything.

At this moment, I am following a vegan diet, seeing an acupuncturist and taking herbs. It isn't easy being a vegan. I have always been a meat eater, and I love cheese. I look at it as a form of cleansing, and I hope that by going a new route, my body will change. I have no idea if it will help me or not, but I am eating healthy, and I am losing some weight. I am not unhappy about this weight loss. I better hurry up and learn to like beans and tofu. If this new approach does not work for me, I will find something else to try. I am tired of being told that nothing can be helped or healed without an enormous amount of medication.

I may be stubborn and wrong, but I have seen how my back straightened despite the doctor's warnings. I managed to get rid of my eating disorder years ago. I have dealt with my emotional difficulties, and over the years I have changed and grown more than I ever thought possible. I got rid of the statins, the antibiotics and the acid reflux medication. I am a lot wiser and less depressed and taken my life and my healing into my own hands. I listen to all the different healers, alternative practitioners and the medical doctors. Then I take what I think I can use and leave the rest. Am I always the right person to make that decision? Maybe not, but I know myself best. I hate to sound like a cynic, but sometimes I wonder who influences the individual practitioners or doctors. Do they follow the advice of the pharmaceutical industry? Is it politically motivated? Many questions and lots of confusion! Who do I trust? I still remember being fooled by a Danish hypnotist. I think that the more desperate I am for help—the easier I am to be fooled. I may do wrong things, but it feels good and empowering to finally trust my own gut. May the angels be with me in this new endeavor!

SLEEP OR LACK THEREOF

Insomnia means that you have a problem falling asleep, staying asleep or waking up too soon. I wish it were that simple. The lack of sleep is an enormous black cloud hanging over me. It has a lot more to do with fear, tension, and dread, not just the mechanics of it. It sounds so easy—you sleep, or you don't. I do not like being in bed—any bed—and my body refuses to relax. It's like having a split personality. My tired soul wants to sleep so badly, but my brain and body can't give in. I have also had restless legs for years. I have learned that Ashwagandha, with its roots from India, can help my legs.

I remember meeting my Danish therapist the first time. I had told her in advance that I wanted to meet her and get to know her before making the decision to work with her. She had to evaluate me to determine if I would be strong enough to work from Switzerland. She had never had a client like me before and didn't want me to fall apart on my way back to Geneva. Her first question was, "Why are you here?" I told her that I hadn't slept in 40 years. She replied, "Then you must be very tired." I loved her on the spot. Finally, someone believed me. She didn't try to diminish my problem or say that it isn't possible. She listened, and our work began shortly after that.

Let us go back a notch. As a small child, I was scared of the dark, and I didn't like going to bed. My brother and I were left alone outside our apartment in a small room off the public hallway. I was not more than a baby or a toddler. I can still feel the loneliness and the fear. Nighttime and darkness became unsafe at a very early age. As I grew up, my fears of the dark grew with me. I remember vivid dreams about wolves with big hateful eyes and they were ready to eat me. My fears of being sent away to live with insane people didn't help. The nightmares set in very early and many of them were repeated night after night.

One dream began when I was about four-or five-years-old. In my dream, I am running away from an insane man. How does a small child know what an insane person looks like? Well…in best childhood fashion, he wore a red hat of course! I would be frantic and eventually hide under my bed. The dream always ended when the man with the red hat slowly looked under the bed. Terrified and with heart pounding, I knew my days were over.

I have been blessed or cursed with very good senses. My sense of hearing is exceptional. Was I born like that or did it develop because I was listening for every footstep, every change in the voices of unlikely intruders? My father was a real night owl. He rarely went to sleep before early morning. Surprise! My sleep difficulties would often disappear around 4:00 in the morning. This has pretty much been the truth all my life. The only problem with that is that I had to get up to take my son to school and get myself to work. I would drag myself out of bed after one or two hours of sleep or sometimes none at all. My fears approached the point of handicapping me. I never dared to go to sleep. Sometimes I would just sit in a chair with pounding heartbeats, waiting for morning to come. Oh…the nightmares, night terrors and the constant need to move around in bed. I think I got more exercise in bed at night than I got during the day. I was not allowed to relax and let go. How can I fall asleep when my whole body is tense, and my brain is scared?

My sleep after 4:00 in the morning was often plagued with bad dreams. In one dream, I was a young adult. Some crazy person opened up my thigh with a surgical instrument and inserted two living rats. They were slowly eating me from the inside, but no one would believe me. I hated that dream and would wake up sweating.

Here are some other dreams that have haunted me.

I only had this dream while I was pregnant.

In the dream, I had just given birth to my little son and was walking in a big green field with my newborn. All of sudden, a trap door opens up in the field. A small door and a staircase lead down into some underground place. Someone pushes my baby and me down into this place. The trap closes and is no longer visible to the world. I was walked down a very long hallway. There were small prison cells on both sides of this long hallway or aisle. A totally insane, half-dead, new mother was in every cell. They all sat on the floor with a baby doll in their laps. In my dream, I realized that I was to be next into one of the cells. I would be given a baby doll, and my newborn baby was to be used for horrible experiments. You could hear the screams throughout the whole place.

I am a baby somewhere between one- and two-years-old and I am as black as the color of death. The scene is a bridge over a river with small towns on both sides. Looks like a nice place. The bridge is high above the water, and there is very little shoulder between the rail and the roadway. In the dream, the baby is placed on the rail on its lower back. Its feet are facing towards the road and head is over the water. The balancing act is brutal and almost impossible, but the fear of falling either way keeps the baby rocking and hoping somebody will come and save it. There is a heavy bracelet around the baby's ankle, which is attached to a chain. The chain is locked onto the rail. Right next to me, also locked to the rail, is a small moneybox with a slot for coins. Now! Anyone who walks by me can put a couple of coins in the box, undo the bracelet and take me off the rail and sexually abuse me. When finished, they would close the lock and hang me back up. I was given a small moment without having to balance on the rail, where I feared falling onto the roadway or hanging on the chain above the water. Saved but not saved. Dead...but not dead. Allowed to live hanging by a thread. No one cares, and there is no need for crying. No one would hear or care.

The cutting of your own hands, halfway between the wrist and the elbow, is scary even if it is only in a dream. I could never figure out why I had that dream. I am quite happy with my hands. They are very capable and can make beautiful things. In the dream, I am forced to cut off both hands. First, I build a guillotine, so I have a tool to help cut off my left hand after my right hand was gone. It was horrifying, and the end scene was a picture of me sitting there on the edge of the bed with arm stumps dripping with blood. It wasn't very painful physically but emotionally; it was more than I could take.

Today I know that this dream has to do with my mother and her stealing of my affection. I will not go into details. I do not have the courage just now, but I have shared with the appropriate people. The first time I shared this dream and its sexual meaning, I was convinced I would have a car crash on the way home. I had done the forbidden and was to be punished. How dare you tell the truth…you filthy little shit? The people around me comforted me for a long time and finally convinced me that I had the right to my truth as I remembered it. For me, it was like I had committed a crime bigger than murder.

This dream I have had very recently.

I am imprisoned by a psychiatrist. I am in a huge compound of some sort and can't escape. There are a lot of people and doctors there, but no one helps me. In the dream, I am a very pretty woman. Every day the doctor is injecting something into my forehead, just above my nose. Slowly, a big sore is developing, and after a while, my skull becomes more and more exposed. It's a horrible face, and it hurts. In my dream, the only way to survive is to kill another person, take his skin and wash it, and color it blue. The blue skin would make me invisible, which is the same as having disappeared from the world. I now know how to stop the abuse from the doctor, but no one will know that I still exist. So, I have to choose between loneliness, terror or the fact that another person will have to die.

I could continue. I could write a whole book about bad dreams. I noticed that, in all my dreams, I am alone…often invisible, scared to death and without hope. Some crazy people almost always abuse me. My father's threat about sending me away to an insane asylum really scared me to death.

This next dream is different from the others. Each and every time I dream it, the details are different, but the essence of the dream is the same.

I am usually the owner of a house or an apartment. There is always at least one room where I am not allowed. Sometimes it is a scary room, other times, an attic filled with old newspapers or a room decorated by somebody else as if it doesn't belong to me. The really scary one is a basement were my mother, father and uncle live. They have their own faces, but their bodies are huge white spiders. I have always been scared of spiders. I sit and worry about the room or basement, and I do nothing else.

Once, during a session, my therapist guided me down the staircase to see what was going on down there. I was shaking, but I kept walking down the staircase. Once downstairs, I met the spiders, and they were holding a much younger me as a prisoner. I managed to save my child self, and as I ran upstairs, the child became a woman. It was a very weird feeling to create a new story like that, but my dream about the basement and the rooms has disappeared.

When I lived alone with my son, I craved people. If I was lucky enough to be invited somewhere, there was a huge problem. I had to come home to an empty dark apartment. It was almost enough for me to say,

"No thanks." Sometimes I did. I so wanted to have a normal social life, but my low self-esteem mixed with this handicapping fear of the dark didn't make it easy. When I opened the door into the apartment while carrying my son, I was almost certain someone would be there. I would try to calm myself down; my ears and eyes were tense, and my heart was beating like a drum. I would put my son to sleep.

My inner alarm system would now be on its highest alert. I could try to go to bed, but sleep would be impossible. Should I—against all the odds—fall asleep, the terrors would strike hard. So yes! Sometimes I did say no thanks to invitations even though I was so lonely. It was much worse when I tried to sleep after coming home in the dark. It was much better if I had stayed home. It didn't help that I held an inner belief that I did not have the right to defend myself. On top of everything else, there was the fear of what would become of my son should something happen to me. The fears were taking over my life, and I was exhausted. When I talk to people about sleep problems, I don't even dare say anything about mine. They have no idea what I am up against. What would they think of me?

After moving to Switzerland, my sleep patterns changed. It was a bit easier to sleep when my husband was home. He traveled an awful lot, maybe 20 to 26 weeks each year. I was often home alone, and now I had a house with three floors to listen to and worry about on these nights. I didn't share a wall with neighbors anymore. When I came home to an empty house after dark, it did weird things to my nervous system. I can't even describe my feeling when I climbed up two flights of stairs to the bedroom. It would have been so easy for me to let the fear take over my life completely, but I had some new friends and that included evenings out. So, I would go. I somehow knew instinctually that if I gave into the fear, it would be over for me. It was already an unimaginable and huge problem, but I wouldn't let it totally and absolutely swallow me. Once in bed, I would lay stiff and listen to the big house.

Of course, there were the nights when I didn't go to bed at all. I would sit in a comfy chair and wait for morning. I always hoped my son didn't notice all this. Children are not stupid, and we never talked about it. I never talked to my husband about it either. It was an absolute necessity for me to keep my fears and embarrassment away from Nick. I was sure he would think I was crazy. His opinion of me was important, and I could not under any circumstances let him see the flawed me. In my warped way of thinking, anything less than perfect was a failure on my part. I carried this fear alone as usual.

When Nick traveled, he would always call home once a day and often early in the morning. I would drag myself to the phone and pretend everything was fine. We were often in different time zones, and it was the middle of the afternoon for him. So, he would chat along for a while. My eyes were closing, and all I wanted to do was to go back to bed. It was especially hard when he called in the early morning on the weekends. I didn't have to take my son to school and could have slept a little. I tried to sound upbeat and happy. I obviously succeeded.

He never knew how little I slept. I felt a lot of shame about my fear. Why can't I get a grip and be like other people? I didn't know of anybody else who had these problems. I had never heard about night terrors except in books. I was sure I was the only one, and if I wasn't, the others were locked up somewhere safe.

One night, maybe seven years after we moved together, an incident happened, and Nick saw my fears and terrors in full bloom. I couldn't hide after that night. In the middle of the night, Nick got up to go into the bathroom. He didn't put on the light, and I didn't hear him. Usually, I heard every little sound in the house—but not that night. Something did wake me up though and, since I was awake, I thought I might as well go to the bathroom. I left the bedroom and just like Nick I didn't think of turning on the light. The moon was out, and I knew my way around. As I walked into the bathroom, I felt and saw a person. My inner children were on their highest alert before my adult brain could think or react. They were 100% sure that this time it was a life or death situation. Instead of freezing, which was my usual behavior, I screamed like I have never screamed before in my life. I ran down the stairs and through the house...like a hunted animal. Nick wondered, "What the heck is wrong with her?" So, then he ran after me.

Now I was really being chased, and I began to scream again. The fear was so huge that my heart could hardly take it. Nick finally got hold of me and convinced me that I had nothing to fear. I was not so sure and was shaking like a leaf. Very slowly, I calmed down. We sat down in the kitchen and Nick poured us a good-sized cognac and demanded an explanation.

I had practically lost my voice from the screaming. I was shame-filled, but I began to tell him the truth about my nightly horrors. He couldn't believe his ears but didn't react in any disrespectful way. There could be no doubt in his mind that my fears were real to me. After all, he had just seen me run through the house, screaming like a wild person. We sat in the kitchen, and I couldn't stop shaking. I was feeling a bit cold from the shock. Nick wanted to put a blanket on me, but it made me feel trapped. I pushed him away...the fear was still lurking under the surface. We eventually finished our drinks. We had calmed down and began to walk back up the staircase. As we walked past the bathroom (*the scene of the crime*), I ran once again. This time not as dramatic and Nick quickly calmed me down. Soon we were back in bed. Nick fell asleep right away, but I couldn't even though I was exhausted to the bone.

From then on, we decided to make some new house rules. No more going around the house without turning the lights on! The next morning I was a bit nervous about seeing Nick again, and my inner children were scared that they were going to be thrown out. We talked it over a little, and fortunately, Nick didn't make a big deal out of it. He now knew my problems and could act with this new information. It was a good feeling to have this secret out in the open. I was worn out. My nervous system had a hard time coming down to normal. My voice was gone for days, and I felt like sleeping for an eternity.

It takes a toll on the body to never get enough sleep. I felt sick and accident-prone. I got the flu, a cold, pneumonia, cuts and bruises all the time. Then the more serious stuff began kicking at my body. I was only 31 when I had the blood clot in my lung and almost died. It made me quit smoking—not an altogether bad thing. I could write tons of pages about the ailments I've had. And I haven't even talked about the muscle tensions from never relaxing.

I am amazed at how much I have managed to do on tiny bits of sleep. We did tons of mountains climbing, hiking, Nordic skiing, tennis and the normal running of a house such as cooking, shopping, etc. Nick was really into extreme sports, and I tried to follow him. Except for mountain biking. I hated the hard work of the uphill. I had problems with all the gears, and I was super-afraid of the downhill. I would brake all the way, and Nick would be miles ahead of me. In December 1999, we tried to climb Mt. Kilimanjaro in Africa. It was an adventure, and it was hard. On the last day and before the summit, I got hit with such bad altitude sickness that I didn't think I would be able to make it down. I had a small swelling on my brain, and it took me years to get over it. The whole ordeal is for another book. I had over-extended my body. It had no more to give.

I kept going and didn't listen to my body. Frankly, I didn't know *how* to listen to it. It was after Kilimanjaro that I began looking for a therapist in Denmark. I was so worn out—beyond tired—and depression was with me again. I was getting to a point where I was afraid of going to bed even when Nick was home. My fear of not falling asleep was ever present. Nick had also begun to snore more than he had before. The whole thing was getting out of hand. When we traveled together and only had one room, his snoring became a big problem, and I didn't have anywhere to go. I would often find myself on the bathroom floor, worn out from lack of sleep. Now I could add the embarrassment of spending the night on bathroom floors. Nick would be so upset at me and often demand that I get back into bed. Then the whole thing would repeat itself.

I was thinking about never traveling again. I was such a hopeless case, and I had tried and failed at sleeping pills. Sometimes I would be so tired that I would just sit down and cry—trying to release stress from my body and soul. Often when I said I would try to take a nap—*I have never been a good napper*—my husband would nap with me. He would fall asleep in two seconds, happily snoring away while I was sitting in a chair sobbing. I began to hate him and his snoring. I'd had enough problems with my sleep as it was.

At home, I would almost always leave our bedroom after my husband fell asleep. I felt guilty if I went into a different room from the beginning; my ever-lasting "friend" guilt was still alive and kicking. I had come to a dead end—exhausted and haunted— hating my snoring husband and myself. It is hard for me to find words to accurately explain how utterly desperate I was then. I needed help. I tried a hypnotist for a while; he was a real quack and cost me a lot of money. I was going to try anything and anybody. So finally, I found Pia, my Danish therapist who believed me. It was almost overwhelming. Tears of release just poured out of my eyes. We had hard work to do, but I had hope.

*Will I ever be a good sleep*er? I shall find that out sometime in the future.

I hope.

SNIPPET TWENTY-FOUR:
HOW TO HEAL?

I had to find the right people at the right time. Then enormous time was spent bleeding my sorrow out—years of telling the same stories over and over again. At the beginning, I only knew that I was second-class, filthy, undeserving, depressed, dirty and ugly. I had kept my early memories under lock and key, also called denial, *My Soup*, misunderstandings and lies. In my brain, there was a lot of confusion as to what went on in my childhood home. I had a hard time trusting myself.

I found a therapist in Nyon, Switzerland. At that point, all I wanted was to be happier—less scared—and to be like everybody else. We spent a lot of time getting to the point of why I was having such a hard time with myself, and the world that I was living in then. I didn't know where it would lead me, but it was while I was with her that I really became aware of my inner children.

I began to acknowledge the emotions of my inner children. It was a strange and new feeling to listen to these sad voices inside me. I had felt my inner children for some years but had not dared to listen to them. I certainly hadn't spoken to anybody about them. I was the only person in the world who was crazy enough to have such an inner life. I was sure of this. I was surprised to find that it isn't that uncommon after all. Could I trust these children and what they were telling me? Firstly, they all wanted to be heard at the same time. Then slowly, I learned to separate them—to feel their ages and individual problems. It had taken a while before I got used to their way of communicating. Secondly, their memories would arise by a smell, seeing a sad child in a supermarket or some loud, angry voices. Other times, the feeling of being a small infant, with its unique set of memories, would surface at the most unwanted moments. One thing was sure. Now that I had begun to listen, I couldn't ever stop again.

I have several inner children. Some are just small voices, while others are very strong and almost have a personality. When they arrive suddenly with all their neediness, they can bring me to my knees. My little baby Kirsten is alone, neglected and afraid of being forgotten. My three- and seven-year-olds are the two children I feel more than the others. They are extremely frightened and fragile. I am beginning to see that often when I react to situations or people around me, it is my small children and their coping mechanisms that react for me. It had never occurred to me that I was emotionally underdeveloped and behaved like a child. It was like being trapped in their limited mindset. If somebody would get upset with me, then my inner core was absolutely sure that this person would degrade and humiliate me as my dad had done. There was no other reasoning. When I think about it all, I am pretty sure my parents were as stunted in their emotional growth as I was. It was very hard to look at myself with such new eyes, and it was not a quick fix. I am still working at it today.

In the pile of letters from my inner children that I have written over the years, I have chosen two: one from my little three-year-old, written when I was about 40 years and another from my seven-year-old, written a few years later. I have translated them from Danish. During this translation, the text lost a lot of the original childish ways of explaining things. It takes a lot of courage to write this, but here it is.

Memory / Letter from a Three Year Old

I think I am about three or four and I am placed on a table. A grown-up man is standing between my legs, which are kicking and moving. He then takes a real hold on me. Iron grip comes to my mind. My legs are held up like you do when you change a diaper. The man makes some weird noises and his eyes glazed over. I try to turn and get away, and I begin to cry. He is strong, and he thinks I am funny. He is laughing at my attempt to escape. I feel dirty, and I do not want to play this game any longer. I need to go potty. I cry harder. I have to pee really bad. It's hard to hold it, but I know it's forbidden to pee on the table, on myself and on this man. I also know that I am a bad girl. I am being punished for something—of that I am certain. I can't hold it any longer, and I begin to pee. It's humiliating, and I am scared. I have peed on everything, and I am afraid of being found in this situation. I am sure I will get into trouble. It's as I am the bad one—the criminal and disgusting person— and not the man who is holding me in an iron grip.

End of Memory / Letter

It is my truth, and I am writing this sad story so that my little inner girl can stop being so scared of somebody coming and holding her in an iron grip. It is part of the monsters she faces every day, and maybe by telling this story, they will go away. Are they really monsters after all—the ones that can walk through walls, fly in through windows and find me wherever

I am? Will the desperate feelings of never being safe or being in danger at all times go away when I can allow my inner children to tell their memories?

I never wanted to believe this story, but I can't ignore it anymore. When I turned over this letter, I realized that I had written some thoughts on the backside. It may have been written some years later.

Dear Angels,

Help me remember more so that I can trust the little one. I know it is disgusting and I feel like vomiting, but I am ready to face it. Together little Kirsten and adult Kirsten are ready. And finally, when I hear her little fine voice, do I believe her. In my family, bad things happened. It is a fact that I have to live with, but hopefully, I will no longer have to be afraid. They can't hurt me anymore. I can't get a clear picture of who it is, but he had easy access to me. I find the whole thing revolting. Everything is embarrassing, and the smells are overwhelming. I have several similar letters to myself. I promise you, it takes guts to write this. My heart is pounding.

Memory / Letter from My Inner Seven-Year-Old

My name is Kirsten, and I am seven-years-old. Everybody calls me Kisser. Right now, I sit next to big Kirsten. I am sitting on the edge of the bed, clad in a dirty, too small and threadbare nightgown. My arms are folded in front of me, and I am both angry and sad. I feel wronged, and I need somebody to talk to, but I don't trust anybody. It's difficult to find help. Help with what exactly? I can't figure this out. I am ugly, and I am different...not like the others. It is now after I have started school that I can see that other families don't live like mine. I meet girls that smell nice and have clean clothes. Their parents smile sweetly, and they speak in a way that I can hardly understand. I feel stupid all the time and don't want anybody—child or adult—to ever meet my parents. I hate that they can see that my parents have no teeth and that my dad doesn't wash too often. I hate that my mother is fat and that she doesn't behave like the other mothers. (As a child, I had a real problem with my mother's size, and that is what I am talking about here. I am not trying to be nasty or hateful to people who are heavy.) I want to be one of the girls that have new clothes and know a lot of things about life. It's embarrassing not to know anything. I really don't know anything, and I am always afraid of the other girls. I hate the boys who tease and hit me a lot. The best way is to pretend everything is fine. Never ask any questions, which will tell the other children how little you know. Don't ever cry, even when they hurt you really bad. Don't cry when they have beautiful, packed luncheon boxes full of good food and fruit. My lunch is not super bad, but every day Susie has a pretty apple with her, and I want so badly to try and taste an apple like that one. I don't dare ask because then she will know that I can't afford such an apple. I don't like it when the others see that my family is poor.

I also know that I hide myself behind my big stupid smile. I hate the dentist, the doctor and myself. The dentist is always angry with me. The doctor is not as bad as the dentist, but I hate when he pulls down my underpants. I don't know what he is looking for, but I know that my underpants are dirty and that is terribly shameful. I don't tell my mother all the bad things from school because my mother can't take anything without crying. Then I have to make her happy again. Telling her would make my problems bigger.

I don't like being naked with other people, but we have gym twice a week. I love the gym, and I am good at it. I hate the showers after gym. I hate them. My mother insists that I wear old-fashioned woolen underpants and the girls at school find them very funny. They see right through me and know that I am different. I try to be really good with my homework. It's neat and pretty. My figures are in straight lines, and I am very good at math. It is getting harder and harder for me to concentrate. I can't relax and feel that people look at me as through a magnifying glass. All my faults get bigger. I try so hard not to be different. I use up all my energy, but I can't figure it out. Who should I be?

When school is over, I walk home. I usually walk with a girl from school, her name is Karoline, and she lives in a really nice big house, not so far away from where I live. She has a beautiful new bike. Sometimes, when I am really lucky, I get to use it a little. She has her own room, and there is always a big bowl of sweets in her room, but she doesn't like to share. She hardly ever takes anything; she isn't interested in sweets and chocolate. I pretend not to want any, but my eyes go towards to bowl all the time. At home, we only get sweets at Christmas. Only my dad is allowed to have candy during the year. My mother eats cake when we are not looking.

On the days when I walk home alone, I am always scared. It isn't far, but I am afraid of child molesters and that kind. Whenever an adult walks towards me, my heart starts to bang really hard. I hurry and cross the street. I turn around all the time. Is somebody behind me? Now, I am almost home, but Uncle Alfred's car is parked downstairs. I know he is sitting having coffee with my mother.

I am never really happy to see Uncle Alfred, even though he is the only one who gives us children some money for a small ice cream. Then I run down to the little store and buy one. I love ice cream.

My dad says that if I was permitted to, I could eat a whole pint all by myself. But of course, it is never permitted. Money. We do not have money, and we have to save on everything. My Uncle Alfred loves my big brother. He had a special nickname for him and often gives him money for ice cream when I don't get any. Sometimes, he gives him enough money to buy a real big ice cream. I would like to have a big ice cream like that, but life is never really fair. My brother doesn't ever share. My uncle loves to tell nasty ugly stories. I don't understand why the adults are laughing. I think he is disgusting. He is not disgusting like my dad because my Uncle Alfred is very afraid of bacteria and things like that. So, he washes a lot. He is a nervous and weird man, and he drinks coffee with my mother a lot. I usually run downstairs to play with my siblings or the other children who live in the same kind of apartment that I live in.

My mother says that all our neighbors have special problems, except us. She says that we are not alcoholics, losers or things like that. So, I am a little different too—even here in my poor neighborhood. I often ask her "Why do we live here where I am afraid of all the adults if we are problem-free?" She says she likes it here. She would be scared of living anywhere else. I think she is afraid of being seen because we also have secrets at home. That secret is about when mother sleeps in my bed. Where is my sister? Who does she sleep with? My sister and I share a small sofa bed, which you can fold away during the day. My mother is very big and takes a lot of space. She sweats a lot, and I don't like her smell. It feels safe and unsafe at the same time. I hate her kisses and her rolls of fat. Why can't she go into bed with dad? What is dad doing? Why do we have to change beds? Is my mother afraid of getting pregnant? Does my little sister get pregnant? When my mother touches me, it's like I am not me at all, but I am my dad. I don't want to play my dad. I just want to sleep, sleep and sleep. When I finally fall asleep, there are big eyes following me—scary wolves—and an insane man with a red hat. They are running after me to kill me. There is nowhere to hide, and I can never ever hide from my mother.

At home, you are never alone. If I close a door and want to be alone for a moment, my mother comes running in and asks if I am sick. She hated closed doors, even the door in the toilet room. When she was home alone with me, she didn't even bother closing the door. My mother sits there with her big fat butt, and I have to see it and be part of it. I don't feel good about it. It feels icky. When I use the toilet, I am always in a big hurry, and I am scared all the time. I keep an eye on the handle. I am not allowed to shower very often, but when I do, I worry all the time that someone will see me naked and laugh at me. I am also scared of being fondled and ridiculed. My father loves to make fun of me, but it isn't fun. It is so sad and awful. I just want to cry.

I don't even remember if my dad ever fondled me, but just the thought is so disgusting, I think I will go and throw up. Is it only my sister? My thinking is like this. My father has my sister. My mother has me. My little brother is too small, and no one cares about my older brother. I sometimes feel very sorry for me. Why can't I have a mother like Susie's mother? She is pretty and nice. I am never scared of her. Sometimes my mother is nice. I love it when I am allowed to comb and set her hair. I am not very good at it, but she likes to be fussed over. Unfortunately, she is too big and clumsy to fuss over me. She never knows when she goes too far...much too far. But she relaxes and looks happy when I comb her hair; my dad thinks we are retarded.

End of Memory / Letter

I have been a bit worried about my inner children's reaction to exposing their very private letters. Perhaps it sounds a bit odd, but I have been given permission to go ahead. *What am I accomplishing by letting it all hang out like this?* The answer is quite simple. I can't carry it alone anymore, and the silence is suffocating me. The silence was necessary for many years, but now I know that the best way to heal is a good amount of truth, daylight and a forceful voice. People's judgment or opinion of me is less important than validation and "being heard." Secrecy, lies, denial and remaining hidden aren't productive. Total honesty about my past and upbringing isn't easy. This includes honesty with myself and others. It is the only way out of self-hate and sadness.

NEW WAYS OF THINKING

I used to react and not think. If I did think, I didn't trust my own thoughts. I used to have feelings just pop-up and overwhelm me. I used to think I had no say in anything. I used to think that I couldn't change. Now, during the healing process, I had to learn to look back at my childhood without judgment. I had to open up new ways of seeing and feeling. *Step back and see the sad little girl without being overwhelmed by her. No more autopilot Kirsten.* My adult brain had to get involved and understand what went wrong and what created the warped thinking and low self-esteem. I had to identify and correct the thinking that went into the beginning and the essence of *The Soup.*

I was never me—the person I was born to be. Other people's feelings were more important, and

I always felt and acted upon them before my own. I would do whatever it took not to be a burden or a problem. Even my speaking became more and more vague. I hoped I could change in mid-sentence in case my antennas noticed any anger or sadness in others. The slightest frown in my father's brow would have me change again. In a split second, my body registered any mood of any person, especially when coming home from play or school. I walked up the staircase to the apartment, and all my spontaneity vanished. I was on high alert and could feel the atmosphere in the apartment—before I entered. As I opened the door, I knew if my mother was depressed, just a little sad or if she had a good day. Had my father teased her to tears? Did she hurt herself in the kitchen again, as she so often did when she was nervous or sad? I could sense if my father was home—in a good or bad mood or in a humiliating superior mood. When entering the apartment, I had already put on the persona who was needed in the moment...to keep me safe and in "control."

As I learned to live accordingly to other people's feelings and needs, I stopped listening to myself. I had sadly lost myself in the process. It just happened. I had become a well-programmed robot. I came to believe that I was here for others and that I was unimportant. That misinterpretation has cost me dearly over the years. I could no longer feel or express my own feelings, and all my energy was used to help other people and assume responsibility for everything bad that happened to everybody else.

As a child, I didn't consciously decide to become a chameleon. For years, I didn't know that life could be any other way. In therapy, I slowly began to know the difference between reacting as usual and reacting on my real feelings, needs and wants. I also began to understand why "my inner children" were reacting as they did. It was difficult to do but necessary for both my mental and physical health.

The memories of my inner children are important in my healing. When allowing myself to validate their stories, I set them and myself free. When I trust my gut and react upon life in an adult fashion, my inner children feel safe and have a lot less need to be heard.

My body also carries the burden, and as a child, I had many physical problems including unending urinary tract and bladder infections, colds, the flu, daily fainting spells, panic attacks, muscle tension, scoliosis, unexplained pains, throat infections and daily headaches. My immune system was weak and couldn't protect me. This is a very big price for holding it all in and letting *The Soup*—and the three big, white spiders with faces of my mother, father, and uncle—win. The spiders will not win.

I mainly write about my small inner children, but I do have a couple of teenagers as well. They see the world in rigid ways, and they are also shamed and abused. They are very shy and embarrassed about themselves. I do not have the same dialog with them as I do with my little ones.

I am still waiting for their stories to be told to me but a lot of that time in my life is forgotten. I have two photos of me as a teenager, and I do not like looking at either one of them—a girl on the heavy side without any confidence. One day, they will begin to speak to me, just like the small ones did...of this I am certain.

When I began to react to the world in new ways or to speak up for myself, it was like having a war inside me. I wanted to change, but the small children were stuck in a different time, and for them, it was a matter of life and death. The message from my three-year-old was clear. *You are going to get sent away. They will hate you.* My nervous system would react like a small child in danger. It was an immediate reaction, and it would happen before I had a chance to realize what was going on. In reality, my inner children were running my emotional life. Their way of reacting to situations didn't fit well into an adult person's life. It took a long time for me to become aware of this and dare to talk about it. Learn why the children felt as they did and finally commit to learning a more analytical and less reactive way of thinking. It couldn't be done as fast as I wanted. If I frightened the children too much, I would be shaken and unwell for days. We were all in it together, and it could only go as fast as everybody could tolerate. We worked on small things in the beginning. You don't have to know everything in an instant, and it doesn't make you stupid to admit to failures and mistakes. No one is going to humiliate and degrade you. If they do, you have the power to walk away. Even when the small ones are scared, you can take control and then comfort them later. As an adult, you can choose not to take any abuse.

This was a freeing and very new way of thinking. It made the world a lot less scary. It was difficult to turn off the old habits…the way of instantly responding. My body and my children definitely did not like the changes. Easy does it.

So, yes. The whole therapy thing is very time-consuming. It was two steps forward and one step back. The negative beliefs I had about myself slowly changed—one small step at a time. Baby steps. My relationship with my son changed too. Baby steps. I was very worried about sending him to college in America. I didn't think he was ready. My therapist told me to mind my own business and look after myself. "The best thing you can do for your son is to take care of yourself, and let him take care of himself." In that way, I would free him up from worrying about his fragile mother. He more than likely thought it was his job to look after me and was not able to deal with himself and his life. It would have ended like me looking after my mother instead of myself. "Trust that he can do it; it's the best gift you can give him." I am glad we ended that bad circle of codependency.

The therapist and I worked together for several years while peeling the proverbial onion. We took off one layer just to find another identical one underneath. It's still an onion, but it's smaller and more manageable.

The process of healing was underway, and I was feeling a bit better. Deep inside my children and I knew that there was a lot more to talk about. There were secrets we had not been able to reveal. The only way I could keep all that away from my everyday life was to deny everything and to make myself into a liar or a crazy person. When I did not allow myself to fully understand and to talk about my secrets, it was like denying myself the right to *be*. I carried a lot of shame, embarrassment and fear. I had internalized my parent's shame; it had become mine. So, with that baggage still hidden, the healing and change could only be limited. I knew that but to honestly talk about the ugly stuff was strictly forbidden. It was forbidden to even think these thoughts, and I had convinced myself that I would rather die than talk. Actually, I thought I would die in a gruesome way, punished for being such a bad girl.

I liked my therapist a lot, but she could not take me where I needed to go, and our work together had to stop. We still saw each other for lunch from time to time, but we had become friends, and the work had ended. I was in need of a therapist who was capable of hearing the stories of sexual abuse and incest. I wasn't ready, and my children were super scared. *What is it about the word forbidden that I don't understand?* A voice inside me would ask me that question. I didn't seek more help for quite a while.

SNIPPET TWENTY-SIX:
MY INNER CHILDREN

I began to read a ton of books, mainly on the subject of incest and sexual abuse. I was obsessed with reading. I literally read hundreds of books in psychology, self-help and many more similar topics. I thought I was going crazy. How could I have such thoughts about my parents and my uncle? I was trying every possible way to deny my own feelings and memories.

I must be the most disgusting piece of shit to have such thoughts. How dare I even think such thoughts and see such pictures in my crazy head. I am sick. Mothers don't do such things to their daughters. Does that make me gay? Am I the bad liar that my mother told me I was? I have no right to feel and think the way I do...filthy bitch.

This self-hate went on and on, and my depression grew with it. My children's stories had to be told, and the next layer of the onion had to be peeled off. My husband supported me, although he had no idea what was going on inside of me and wondered why I needed more therapy. No one knew how I struggled. I always pretended life was great and managed to do a ton of things while my inner children were crying and screaming at me. I didn't want to hear them and their filthy stories, but the war between us was making me emotionally and physically sick too. I had to listen. I had to hear my own story no matter how hard it would be for me. I would never be well without it. My early wounds were open and oozing.

It was clear to me that I had to find a therapist in Denmark. My inner children didn't speak anything but Danish, and they wanted to be heard. A girlfriend in Denmark began to ask around for me and quickly found a therapist. She thought I would like her. I went to Copenhagen to check her out and liked her on the spot. We found a way to deal with the distance, and I jumped in with both legs. Pia's way of therapy was very different. It was almost like being invited into a private home, and she always made a big pot of tea for our two hours together. It was like visiting a girlfriend. She never took notes but never forgot anything. I often wondered if there was a hidden microphone somewhere, but I do not believe so. She made my inner children very welcome and sensed which one was present.

Let me clarify here. I do not have multiple personality disorder. My children are with me, but I am also there. I do not ever remember a moment when I had to leave for a child to be present. My children are very real to me, and sometimes when I am really stressed, they show up with all their emotions and fears and want to take over. It's like being an adult and at the same time having childish emotions, wishes and wants. When I was with Pia, my children came out in a way that I had never seen before. We had to make an important agreement. While driving, the children were not allowed to be present and there was days when it was impossible for me to drive.

It would happen like this. I would begin to talk about a situation in my memory bank, Pia would ask questions and, all of a sudden, the child who carried the memory would let me feel with all my senses— how it had been for her at the moment it actually happened. It was exhausting and after two hours. I was tired to the bone. We would usually work for five or six days in a row. I wanted change so much, but there were days when I had had enough. I felt so drained, but we kept on going. I usually stayed with a girlfriend. My family didn't know that I was in Denmark. I could not cope with the therapy and my dysfunctional family at the same time. It was hard to be so close to my little nephews and my niece without saying hi to them.

As I listened to the children and began to believe them, I found an inner strength. I had survived all that stuff and carried it alone for so many years. I had not turned into an alcoholic, drug addict or gone mad. I was indeed stronger than I had ever given myself credit for or believed. Allowing my story to be told and having a caring witness is very empowering. No more hiding. No more secrets. It became easier for me to feel sadness and understanding of myself than to feel hate. I was beginning to grieve. I was grieving the childhood that I didn't have, and I was crying for all the time that I had wasted in *The Soup*.

Sad and angry, I also grieved over the years I had spent blindfolded in *The Fog*—*The Fog* that prevented me from seeing and understanding the truth about myself. I was grieving with every one of my inner children. They are so incredible, sad and helpless. This grieving period took a long time. I cried as hard as if I had lost a loved one. And in a sense, I had lost several loved ones. I was wondering how much sadness I could take before fell to pieces. I had stopped seeing my sister and my mother years before, and I was also grieving that loss. Sometimes, I wished I could go home to Denmark and have a lovely Danish Christmas with the whole family. I had chosen to get away from the dysfunction, but it was a big price to pay. I missed my sister and even my parents at times. I missed the good part of them but did not know how to be around them. I was always afraid of my mother's neediness and victim behavior. I was afraid of my sister's tongue. My inner children were always on high alert around my family, and they had to come first in my priorities.

Pia was very good at pushing me along—not too much but enough to see progress. I don't remember how many weeks we worked together, but we were together for several years. During that period my self-hate almost stopped. My children became less and less scared and needy. Towards the end of my time with Pia, we decided to give the children the peace we thought they needed. I wrote a thank you note to each one of them. *Thank you for carrying all the pain. Thank you for being strong and lots more.* I put the letters into an envelope and sealed them. Then we had a little burial ceremony. My inner children had done their job and Pia, and I were coming to an end. Pia and I also became friends after the therapy was over and, when I am in Denmark, I love having lunch with her. Just like being with and old friend. I was actually fun to get to know her as a private person and not a counselor.

I had done it. I had talked about the forbidden— maybe not all of it—but I had dared to open up to the most hurt and sad parts of me. The world had not come to an end. I still wasn't ready to share my story outside of therapy, except for a few girlfriends.

My husband knew more and more about the inner children and their stories. It felt good to have him on my side. I also finally really moved into my house in Switzerland—the one I had lived in for years. I began to demand changes to it. It wasn't always Nick's way or the highway anymore. Earlier, I thought he was bossy and controlling, but I have learned that I was also at fault for thinking that I had no right to stand up to him. How could he know about my needs and wants when I didn't dare tell him anything about them?

I remember he once said to me, "Being married is not supposed to be a guessing game." I got a little mad, but then I realized that it must have been hard maneuvering around me. I was the one who never dared to show myself to the world. I tried to get better. He wasn't always super-thrilled with all my wishes and all the changes, but all-in-all we were happier. At least I was.

Sometime before beginning to live in my own house, I had a most wonderful dream. I was back in the dream about forbidden and scary rooms and haunting basements. This time I walked downstairs to the basement. To my amazement, I found an oversized garage filled with beautiful cars and areas for fun, leisure and creativity. My secret rooms that had held me back with fear had finally opened up to greatness. I felt hopeful. I had changed a basement full of fear and terrible spiders to a garage filled with opportunities and fast cars! This was a big deal for me. I was finally living in my own house, feeling my own feelings and not hurting my body on purpose anymore. I remember thinking that I maybe I had some potential. There was definitely something new brewing in my spirit.

My husband liked the new and stronger me. He loved to see me more assertive, except against him of course. He was and still is a big support and help for me. I totally trust him, and I know he would never do anything to hurt me. We have had our moments. He was so used to a more subservient Kirsten, and now he was married to someone who began to demand things. He always manages to change with me. He changed at a slightly slower pace than I did, but he was always willing to try to help me. Thank God for that. In therapy, you learn a different language, and it was sometimes hard for him to understand exactly what on earth I was talking about. I would get frustrated when he couldn't see things as clearly as I could. It isn't easy to change and do the work, but it is all worth it.

I still had my demons. My low self-esteem was somewhat of a problem. It was not like in the old days, but it was still there. Overall, I felt a lot better and more at home in my own body. I used less energy in worrying about what others might think.

Unfortunately, my night terrors and my fears of the dark did not go away.

Therapy has been a wonderful tool for me. Reading books and writing to myself have also been helpful. I have been writing for years, not a journal exactly, but a piece of paper whenever something needed to be told, and there was nobody to trust. My inner children have written many pages over the years. I still have a hard time with some of their writings. Over the years, I have written down sentences or poems I would find interesting or eye-opening. I have always kept my writing in a pretty, secret box, which I had hidden away.

I was concerned that somebody would find it. Most letters to myself were obviously in Danish, but some were not. Sadly, I have lost a bunch over the years. I hadn't seen or touched many of these writings for years. I read them all again while preparing for this book. I can still feel the sadness and despair.

The Poem

Here is a poem that I copied from a book. As far as I remember, the author was anonymous:

Lonesome Detention

You laughed at my weaknesses – therefore I
    was afraid of showing them
You trampled on my dreams – therefore I
    dreamt alone or stopped having any.

You were too busy to listen – therefore I didn't
    speak
You weren't discreet with my secrets – therefore
    I didn't share them with you.

You were insensitive to my needs – therefore I
    hid them from you
You never understood anything – therefore I
    stopped trying to communicate.

You injured me with your indifference –
    therefore I bleed inside
You only met my physical needs – therefore
    my soul is impoverished
You forced me into myself – therefore I am
    now in prison.

My inner teenager loves that poem, and we go back
to it often.

I learned many important things by reading book
after book. Self-love is not egotism. Egotists hate
themselves but act as though they are God's gift to
mankind. They show off, brag and pretend to be who
they fear they are not. This was an important find for
me as I had always wondered that if I should get well
enough to actually love myself would I then be a self-
ish egotist. But don't worry! I am not there yet.

I had begun to learn a whole new way of thinking
and understanding. I was learning the language of

healing—being honest and truthful about who I am, even if it is difficult.

It all sounds so fantastic, and I thought I was done with therapy forever. I was "cured," my inner children buried and my core was so much stronger. I had finally gotten myself out of *The Soup*.

MORE LETTERS

Letter from my Letterbox, Written on a Bad Day, December 2002

Loneliness…it's still with me. How my childhood wounds haunt me today. Can I ever change my feelings of unworthiness?

My core is still so very hurt. My stomach and neck areas are always tense. It's impossible to relax at all. I do not know who I am… just a girl in hiding. Nobody hears me, sees me or cares for me—especially me. I am just too unimportant to take any space in this world. As a child, I thought that even my breathing took too much space and was too loud. It made noise when the lungs moved in and out. I tried to teach myself to breathe as quietly as possible.

Can I ever give up believing this weird paradox? If you are a bad girl, they will see you and deal with you. If you are a good girl or have success, they will see you and deal with you as well. To be somebody...that is dangerous. To be smart...that is not desired. It's best to pretend to be an invisible nobody. I got better and better at it. Today is one of those days when it hurts a lot. Sometimes success and failure take me to the same spot.

I do remember a picnic with my family and my mother's half-sister and her husband. I was about five-years-old. Some inner anger wanted to test my mother's commitment to me. Can I only receive food or attention if I have been useful first? Would she give me food just because I was there? Would she have such a good time for herself that she would forget me? *A mother is supposed to feed her children.* I knew that but would she feed me? She did forget me, and I stubbornly didn't ask for food. This was my way of testing my mother and my situation. On the way home, my young stomach was screaming with hunger. I told her that I had not been offered any food. My mother reacted with such shame and almost began to cry. I felt like the most horrible conniving little brat. The feeling of being so unfair to my mother haunted me for years. (I still write about it years later). I hadn't given her a chance, but my need to test her was too big to ignore. How stupid of me! Now I had to be a mother for my mother again. I knew already that she couldn't cope. She was a hurt animal just as I. The only difference was that it was ok for her to be weak and needy, whereas I had to hide my problems. If I didn't tiptoe around her, she would be overwhelmed, and I would feel awful. I tried to suppress my need for fun, my need for ambitions, and even my need for life. This test was my little girl's rebellion. I never did something like that again. Things had a way of backfiring.

I always play the happy girl. The all-knowing girl who has no need for questions. Fake it and do it well. It is very lonely to be me—with the stupid grin and the confident role-playing. Anything to hide my fears and inadequacies. Hide, so nobody can ever see how lonely you are.

Regards from the tense stomach.

Signed,
THE VERY LONESOME GIRL...NOW A WOMAN

End of Letter

Letter to myself written about twenty years ago.

Even if you can't afford anything, you can still wish…wish for the best of everything.

I have just read this sentence, and it makes me think. How would it be to grow up in a family with this belief? Then everything is possible, and there is hope. The fundamental problem in my family was that my parents didn't believe we deserved anything. It wasn't the fact that we were poor. It was impossible to write a wish list for Christmas. "Kirsten, what do you wish for? Is it gifts or hopes for the future?" If I ever acknowledged a wish, then I would surely be cursed…never to receive anything. It's almost beautiful how smartly they set me up. If you don't dare to wish for anything, then they don't have to ever say no to you. Teach the children to have no needs and wants.

Imagine knowing that the best is possible and you are allowed to wish for it or to believe that dreams are okay. Not moderate in anything, even in my fantasies. It's like a door is being opened…just a crack…but it's there. You are allowed to wish for the best. It doesn't mean that you will get everything but the mere fact that you are allowed to wish for everything. You didn't earn it or deserve. You just wish. Wow.

I lived for 40 years without knowing that you didn't have to limit yourself. I get totally dizzy over the enormity of this new thinking. Then there are no stopping thoughts, dreams, creativity—and life. This could set me free. The straight jacket is loosening its grip.

Maybe I don't have to feel guilty when I buy something that makes me happy. One thing is for sure. You'll never get the best if you don't even dare wish for it.

I will start wishing today!

End of Letter.

SNIPPET TWENTY-EIGHT:
TOO MUCH MOTHER

I t's not only my small inner children who have memories that they would like to forget. The dysfunction in the family obviously didn't stop just because I grew up. As a child, I didn't know any better. As an adult, it became harder and harder to live with the secrets and the pretend.

I always was afraid of setting boundaries with my mother. (In honesty, I didn't know what boundaries were until after some therapy.) I was very frightened of hurting her, as it was my job to keep her happy. I had also been brought up with the indoctrination that she was a very fragile woman. But there was a much bigger problem—or maybe I should call it absurd thinking. *How could I ask my mother to stop getting physical with me, when we both pretended it didn't happen?* We never acknowledged it and never spoke of it. In a sad, strange way, I was trying to keep any embarrassment away from my mother—even though she was the one who was doing the embarrassing stuff. I somehow carried the blame and the shame. I was still trying to protect my mother...it was my duty. Often, when I am in denial mode, I wonder if it was all just a bad dream. For many years, I had it all hidden away behind sickness and *The Fog.*

As I grew older, I didn't know any better how to deal with the situation, but I got a little smarter around her. I always entered her apartment with arms full of things. There was no free space for a hug. I did the same thing when I said goodbye. When together, I tried to try not to sit next to her, and I always had a reason why as she was very demanding. I remembered to avoid certain subjects as they could trigger her. And on and on it went. As much as I wanted a close relationship with my mother, it couldn't happen. I had to live this life of pretending. Frankly, for years I thought I was a bad girl for finding my mother icky. We were utterly enmeshed and without boundaries. It couldn't change.

Even as an adult, she would touch me in ways that were embarrassing to me, and she would speak to me about things that I didn't want to know. I still pretended it didn't happen. I think I was hoping that if it wasn't mentioned or "felt," I didn't have to deal with it. I felt inadequate and childish in my few and small attempts to make her stop. I fully believe to this day that she didn't have any idea about personal integrity. I was her daughter, and to her, it meant that we were one and the same.

One episode still stands out, and I can remember in detail how I felt at that moment. I was visiting my parents. It was the first time I had my now husband-to-be with me. I was a little apprehensive since my parents didn't speak English and for other good reasons. My dad didn't speak English at all, but my mother made a real effort. (She actually began to take English lessons so she could better communicate with Nick). My mother had set a very nice coffee table and had baked a very good coffee cake. I was translating back and forth. My parents and Nick didn't have a lot in common, but we all tried to have a good afternoon together. We were on our best behavior, or so I thought until…I do not know how it happened…but I ended up sitting next to my mother. All of a sudden I felt her hand walking up my bare back under my blouse. Her hand got under my bra strap and began to caress me from side to side. It was normal behavior for her. I was mortified. *Is this mindless or is she showing some form of ownership?* I didn't want Nick to see this happening, and I became stiff as a rod. I wanted the floor to open up and swallow me. All I could think of was, "How can I stop this without him knowing what is going on?"

I couldn't tell how long it actually lasted—it felt like hours. I was crying on the inside. I promised myself that I would never ever sit next to her again. I never did. Thank God! Nick didn't notice. I would have died in shame.

For many years, I tried to have as normal a relationship as I could with my mother. I needed a mother and later a grandmother for my child. She needed a daughter that would take care of her every need in perpetuity. We never talked about our dysfunction or faced up to and dealt with it. In the end, it was easier to stay away from her than to ever talk to her about it. How could I speak to my own mother about the unspeakable and the secrets? It was like it would take away that part of her that was good to me. I couldn't separate the good from the bad. I guess that is what enmeshment really means. In order to have some good memories of her, I had to never talk about the bad. In the end, it meant no relationship at all.

SNIPPET TWENTY-NINE:
NEEDING HELP AGAIN

We loved Albuquerque, New Mexico and the friendly atmosphere there. My health kept deteriorating, and I was popping pills as I had never done before. The straw that broke the camel's back was the Addison's disease. At first, I thought I was developing Alzheimer's disease. I couldn't remember normal things. I never felt well, and the depression was creeping in again. My husband, who is 23-years older than I am, was in a lot better condition. I loved it for him, but I hated being a sick, whining woman with something to complain about every moment of the day. He listened and he cared, but it couldn't have been easy. I was hoping that moving to a lower altitude in Tucson, Arizona would help.

I tried to concentrate on a move that I didn't even want. This was awful. It broke my heart to say goodbye to everybody. I ran out of energy all the time—I could feel myself sliding down into the old negative, self-hating me. It was lonely living in Tucson. People weren't as immediately friendly as the folks in Albuquerque. It took a long time for the Addison's disease medication to be properly regulated. Once that was done, some of my symptoms disappeared.

My physical self was getting a bit better. Why didn't I get happier? I couldn't believe it, but I was in need of a therapist again. The move and the disease had brought me to my knees, and my old wounds were bleeding again. It seemed to me that they would never end. The old ways come back and haunt me over and over again. How many layers does this onion have?

One more time, I was looking for a therapist. I was recommended to go see Jean who was more of a professional counselor and very different from Pia in Denmark. *I miss the tea.* Jean takes notes and has tons of tools up her sleeve. She is very knowledgeable and has a sweet, caring personality. Jean is not the kind of counselor who wants you to stay with her for years on end. She wants you to be well, and she will find the fastest way. She has introduced me to so many new and interesting ways to work on my healing. I am very impressed with her skills. She has managed to find strength in me. *I didn't know I had it.*

First, she introduced me to *EMDR* or *E*ye *M*ovement *D*esensitization and *R*eprocessing. It's quite a mouthful, but so far it has worked well for me. It is a technique that is very helpful for people with *PTSD* (*P*ost-*t*raumatic *S*tress *D*isorder). I would not know how to begin to describe the psychology behind it, but I can tell you how it works for me.

As you already know, one of my major problems is night terrors. Another problem of mine is my core belief that I am not just incapable of defending myself—nor allowed to do so. These beliefs remain firmly in place and the night terrors and other fears can really knock me off my feet. My body went into a total freeze, and I became a little, helpless creature. My old reactive patterns are in charge at night, and they do not let the adult assess the situation. There is no will power. *I am a quivering glob of jelly.* It's like a *small death* every time. My fears make for a good *EMDR* subject.

As we began to work together to relief me of my constant barrage of fears, we discovered that I needed the voices and the memories of my inner children. These were the same inner children my Danish therapist, and I had buried, in good faith, years ago. We believed in that moment that these sad children needed peace, but now I needed them back to help me. With some fear in my stomach, I went home to find the Thank You letters that I had written to each one of them. Years had gone by, but I knew exactly where they were. They were inside an envelope in my secret box, hidden away in a safe place. I had never been able to burn or bury those letters. I made sure I was home alone and opened the envelope. I read each letter while heavy tears were streaming down my cheeks. It was almost instantaneous; they were back. I could feel all their emotions and memories come flooding back. I was overwhelmed with it all, and it took me a while before I could compose myself. I sat on the floor for a couple of hours. I was still a bit fragile when my husband came home. I didn't mention any of this to him. It was too personal, and I was worn out. The next day, I translated each letter into English so my therapist could read them. I didn't know how important it was for her to hear them, but I wanted her to fully understand how much I cared for these children. They were holding the memories for me, when I was too weak or stressed to be able to see, or when denial was stronger than anything else. The inner children might have been little and sad, but they have also been strong...they survived it all and went into hiding with it.

Now I had my inner children and all their memories and fears with me, and the EMDR session could begin. My therapist told me that all I had to do was to follow her fingers with my eyes. She would move her fingers from side-to-side, and I would move my eyes to her rhythmic finger movements. It's a little like being in a trance—but fully awake at the same time. We had chosen a memory to work on, and I was told to let go. The therapist said, "Just let whatever comes to mind enter. Don't judge anything. Feel the emotions that come." When the dread and horror came flooding over me, she would give me valuable tools that really helped with the work. She taught me about creating a safe place inside myself. We discovered a caring and nurturing mother inside me. I had my angels and my Higher Power. As I went deeper into my fears, I became more and more scared and agitated. She would remind me to use the necessary resources. We changed the story and created a new and safer space. As I felt safer, I would continue my progress and deeper and deeper—until I met the deepest and darkest side of my fears. I had never dared to go to these places. Then, all of a sudden and out of nowhere, I found a strong male voice inside me.

He didn't take any shit from anybody. It was a wonderful find…he wasn't scared of anything. Contrary to my old way of thinking, since he was male, he had the right to defend himself—me. I became aware that being a woman in my brain had been equal to being totally helpless and defenseless.

My childhood belief was beginning to change and I was now ready to defend myself. Life becomes a dangerous place when you aren't allowed to take care of yourself, to stand up for yourself or to defend yourself. I am ready now.

I was speechless and overjoyed. I felt that God had handed me a gift. Shortly after this knowledge entered my consciousness, I had to be home alone. *Funny how that works.* It happens every time I discover something new. There is an almost instant reason to try it out in real life. My husband was going out of state and, as usual, I was nervous about the nights. For the first time—I really mean the first time in my life—I did have a night alone without night terrors or nightmares. I didn't get tons of sleep, but I wasn't scared. I felt like I was newly released from prison. I was with my newly found inner male and ready to do battle...ready to do whatever it took. I knew I could hurt someone if necessary. At first, I thought I would have to...well sort of...call upon him. I soon realized that he was just a part of me—a part that I couldn't see earlier. My parents' lies about helpless women and my mother's belief that women can only be victims were no longer true. After the first night without terrors, I sat on my bed and smiled to myself. *I am taking in the victory lap. I have finally won over my worst fears.* I thought it was too good to be true but the second night was also without the old haunted feelings. No one was coming to torture, rape and kill me. If they did, I had my own God-given right to defend myself.

Another time we were working on a memory of mine—being in bed with my mother—I also got wonderful help from my male self.

It was a sad scene. I was in my dirty nightgown and very frightened. Shame filled the room. It was a very emotional, strong scene. We asked my angel to be there so I could feel strong enough to go on with the work and not crumble or fall apart. Jean asked me to find my inner male. I needed his help. In my trance or fantasy, he came storming into the room, with the door smacking open. He asked, "What the hell is going on here?" His energy overpowered everyone. He took my little inner girl by the hand and walked out of there.

I had created a powerful ending to a sad memory. I will never forget the last scene. The tall, strong male was holding hands with the girl, and the angel wrapped her wing around her. Together they walked out of the house. I only saw the back of them and like seeing a real film, I saw on top of them. The End.

I could almost hear the music playing too. I began to laugh. It was so funny, and the memory had no hold over me anymore. I looked up at Jean and said, "The shame belongs to the fat lady." We both found that sentence very funny and healing.

It was a good sentence. "The shame belongs to the fat lady." As I drove home, I began to think about what this actually meant for me. It was that being so shameful made me want to disappear. I was afraid that people could see my shame. I have had a hard time with eye contact. I had made a choice very early on that I was invisible and in hiding. I thought that others made a choice not to see me or hear me; they didn't want to know me. I believed they didn't want to be with me because I was damaged and less-than. It has finally dawned on me, that I am the one in hiding. I am the one who believed I was damaged and unworthy and I project that out into the world with my behaviors. Inside me, I knew I was bad. Why otherwise was I treated so? I had internalized my mother's shame and carried her shame. I came to believe that I wasn't worth anything...just as she was worthless in her own eyes.

I have spent 50 years or more of my life hiding myself and keeping my story from the world. I was convinced that if people knew my past, they would be disgusted with me and that everyone would believe that I was making it up. I was living the safe way, or so I thought. I became invisible and didn't belong in the world by not sharing the real me with anyone. Since I have begun sharing, I have learned that when I own my past and myself, I become a human being like everyone else. When I share bits of myself, people do not run away but instead find me courageous. If I tell my story, people want to hear more, and I become somebody. If I sit back and pretend that everything is fine, I become invisible, and no one will see me. I get what I dish out. This is so incredibly contrary to what I have always believed. I have overcome the hurdle in my warped thinking… the belief that telling my truth makes me a liar. It shouldn't shame me to see my truth in its own light. It should shame the people who shamed me. Of all people, my mother gave me buckets-full. I took it, carried it and went into hiding.

Jean and I have worked on many memories this strange way. What haunted me has less and less power over me. Jean puts me in control of my own thoughts, and together we give sad and scary stories happy endings. I know it sounds weird, but it works. That's all I need to know. I was introduced to the right tools and learned. I learned so much about the wonderful healing power of my brain.

As I write all this down, I also know that I am a lot healthier and stronger than I make it sound on paper. In therapy, I am dealing with old emotions and memories that are still stuck inside me. I react in old patterns and do regress from time-to-time. It doesn't mean that I can't function in the world. The old coping patterns stay in the therapy room and hardly ever interfere any more with my everyday life.

Today, when I am my normal self, nobody would ever guess what I have gone through with my demons and sleep problems. Even fewer would believe that I still struggle with a lot of monsters and self-esteem problems. In general, I am a smiling and mostly happy person. I go about my life in an organized and orderly fashion. I cope better and better with life's situations. I do not worry as much as I used to, but depression and sadness can still hit me. Whenever it does, my old isolation and hiding patterns kick in—smiling on the inside, and you know the drill...

Jean is also very hot on group work. In the past, my stance on group work was, "Don't waste my time. Why on earth should I want to be involved with other people's problems when I can't even deal with my own stuff?" She was also right here. I have met some very nice women, and when we share and care for each other. It's like having the mother I never really had. I will not go into any detail for obvious reasons. These women have not been asked to be in a book and should be treated with respect. As with everything, honesty and bravery are the roads to healing, and these women want it as much as I do.

SNIPPET THIRTY:
CO-DEPENDENTS
ANONYMOUS

S hortly after meeting Jean, she talked about something called *Co-D*ependents *A*nonymous (CoDA).
*Co-dependents Anonymous is a fellowship of men and
women whose common purpose is to develop healthy relationships. We gather together to support each other in a
journey of self-discovery—learning to love the self. We have
each experienced in our own ways the painful trauma of the
emptiness of our childhood and relationships throughout
our lives. We attempt to use others—our mates, our friends
and even our children—as our sole source of identity, value
and well-being, and as a way to restore within us the emotional losses of our childhoods. We have all learned to survive life, but in CoDA we are learning to live life. Through
applying the Twelve Steps and principles found in CoDA,*

we can experience a new freedom from our self-defeating lifestyles. No matter how traumatic your past or despairing your present may seem, there is hope for a new day in the program of Co-dependents Anonymous. May you find here a new strength within to be that which God intended – Precious and Free. (This is taken from Co-Dependent Anonymous Newcomers Handbook.)

I reacted just as I had with the group work but Jean insisted that I try it out. I only went to please her, and I hated the first meeting. I didn't like one person there. I didn't like what they were talking about. I didn't like the format of the meeting. I left in a mixture of sobbing and anger. They had given me a stupid little welcome chip. I threw it out of the car window on my way home. I was never ever going back to this stupid CoDA meeting again—period!

As always, Jean got her way. She begged me to go just one more time. It took a lot of courage to do so, but I am very happy that I did go. The second time was a lot easier and, for some reason, the people there were a lot more welcoming than they had been on my first day. I was listening intently and really began to hear the stories of other people at the meeting. Then, I was telling some of my story. It was so freeing and humbling. No one there is out to get you. There is a lovely understanding and caring atmosphere. It takes some getting used to—telling a bunch of strangers your most inner thoughts, but it works.

CoDA is a safe place where I meet like-minded people. We all have at least two things in common: dysfunction in our primary family and a need to be needed, loved or to be "used" by other people. We somehow do not deserve to be here on earth without *giving* all the time. Often, we extend ourselves to the point of exhaustion. We give advice, help and take over whether people want our help or not. If I am not needed or can be of use, then who am I? *Just being me is not enough.* I have to justify my every move. It's not something I was really conscious of until I began to go to CoDA meetings. In the meetings, people share and tell about themselves, and it is surprising how open and honest they are.

I was new to CoDA, maybe a couple of months, when a young woman told this story: *"I do not know why I treat other people like small gods. Right now, I am in a bad relationship. I know it is bad. He doesn't treat me well at all and he is often abusive. Once he tried to strangle me. I will do anything to deserve his love. I will massage his feet and be his slave in hope of his love and acceptance of me. I do not know why I do this and I know it has to stop. How do I stop it when I feel that I do not deserve any better?"* What a sad and desperate place to be—not to deserve anything at all. (Note: This woman gave me her permission to share this story in my book.)

I could see myself in those feelings but maybe not in the details. Before CoDA, it never occurred to me that I allowed other people to become gods over me—gods that could judge me, decide for me, treat me as they pleased or tell me what to do. I would let it happen. The closer people were to me emotionally, the more I created that scenario. It never entered my brain that I was doing this to myself and not them. I am not giving everybody a pass for trying to get me to do these things, but I am the one who let it happen. This is the problem. I had learned to sit back and take it, and I had learned well. Luckily, it is never too late to take notice and begin to change.

Hiding emotions is another topic that shows up a lot in our meetings. I personally can feel sad and angry, but it never comes to the surface. My need to be loved and never ever hurt anybody would stand in the way. I misunderstood the world! If I disagreed or maintained a really firm opinion, it was equal to actually hurting somebody else. I am always scared of the tears of other people. I think I am at fault. It would be up to me to make people happy again. It was as if my mother's tears are following me around and haunting me. I lived this sad, misunderstood life and thought it was everybody else who created it. When people really didn't deserve my love, I tried even harder. I wanted everybody to like me and to love me—anything but don't abandon me. I did not validate my own needs and wants if they interfered in the slightest with the happiness of others. I tried to please everyone so much that I end up resenting the very people I was trying to help. It is part of the crazy *Soup* thinking.

It is often the small things that really matter to me. Let's say my husband is telling me what to do in a specific situation. *Doesn't he think I know anything? Does he think I am stupid and that I can't make my own decisions?* On the outside and in a low voice I say, "Don't tell me what to do." When he brings it up again and again, I begin to crumble. I go silent. On the inside, I am very angry, but he doesn't know that. He might even think that my silence means that I agree with him. I feel trapped. I think I have to do what he wants or his feelings will be hurt. Also, his opinion is more valid than mine. Doing what he wants me to do will make me feel like a small child who doesn't dare to stand up for herself. I could also choose to go ahead and do what I had already planned to do. This would hurt his feelings or make him angry with me, and that is forbidden in my world. There is a third option. Pretend that it isn't important and bury it down in the pit in the stomach—the pit where I store forgotten, hurt feelings brewing in acid. I often chose the third option. It's the easiest at the moment, but it adds to the self-hate and the anger. Sometimes it is difficult to be a loving wife, especially when the anger in the pit is brewing.

Small things should be forgotten and forgiven, but it is not really the details that make me so angry. It's the feeling of being trapped that makes me feel like a coward and a weakling. How do you get rid of all these bad emotions so that they don't fester and turn into bitterness? The more I hate and disrespect myself, the less I can stand up for myself and act like an adult. I keep adding to the pit of "forgotten hurt and angry feelings," a pit that began somewhere in early childhood. It's part of my *Soup*. The belief that I am important and have as much right to my opinion as everybody else was slow in coming.

After the situation has past and my husband begins to notice my silence, he wants life to go back to normal. He gives me a hug, and often I pretend that everything is fine. On the inside, the whole house has collapsed. I feel like running away, and I hate myself for yet again being such a coward. Then life goes on until the next small situation arrives and the whole dance starts all over again. It's an unhealthy way of living. All the hurt and shame have become parts of my nervous system and me. It manifests itself in physical pain.

Sometimes when I try to explain these things to my husband, he looks at me like I am insane. "Why on earth do you let such small things bother you?" For me, it's not really the actual situation and the specific details. It's the feeling of being stuck. I can't speak up to him. I am way too worried about his thoughts and feelings to recognize my own. The fear of being seen as wrong, needy, less-than-others and of course my big fear—if someone thinks that I am insane—is terrifying to me. The fear of being *thrown away* sits in my bones—so deeply ingrained from childhood—that my inner children's voices are louder than my adult voice of today. I know it sounds silly, and I get it on an intellectual level, but when the fear comes, the brain goes out of the window. To be thrown out. I don't even know what it would look like in my adult world of today. The inner children only know one thing, and that is fear. So hurry up and be whatever it takes for this bad moment to go away.

I had thought that all the old thinking patterns were dealt with, but they are still there but to a lot lesser degree. I am opening up and learning more. It is so healing and rewarding to finally say things out loud. I love to be sharing with normal everyday people and not just paid professionals. I am not diminishing the therapists that I have worked with. There is a real difference for me between sharing my memories out in the real world as opposed to the total safety of anonymity in a therapy room. When the pain inside me dares to come out into daylight, and no one thinks less of me, the healing can begin.

I slowly open up for old wounds and memories and change can begin to happen. When people hear and see me with all my faults and don't hate me. I slowly see myself with all my faults and do not hate myself either. This is the slow work of CoDA.

So here is a paradox for you. I obviously don't see myself as others see me. I hear that from friends and family all the time. They tell me that I am very forceful and super-frank. Some people find me almost coarse and too direct. They see a totally different personality than the one I see. Yes...I can see where they can get the idea. I do have a frank side to me. If my inner children don't feel threatened, I can relax and just be me. At social gatherings or on the tennis court, I feel safe. I enjoy the more forceful me. I have lived with so much confusion and deceit in my life that I can't stand it. I try to respect myself and the people around me and maintain an honest approach. I tell it as I see it and I can be opinionated. I do have a good sense of humor. Thank God—otherwise, life wouldn't have been tolerable. It is also amazing what you can say with a big happy smile on your face.

People get a lot less offended when you put an arm around them, smile and proceed to tell them the bare truth. I am also a very organized person and take charge of things if no one else comes forward. I have noticed in CoDA that the outside persona often doesn't resemble the sad inside. It's not just me. We all carry around a facade and mine is a happy, strong one.

I remember coming to America and seeing the reaction that I got from the women here. They didn't like my directness. They got used to me and certainly knew where I stood. No hidden agenda and no deceit. I never hurt anyone on purpose. If it happened that I did hurt people, I wished people would tell me right up front that I had hurt them so that I could make amends. Most people just don't do that. Instead, they tell their hurt feelings to several friends. This never solved anything.

I know this scenario very well. I lived that way for many years and can still do it. It depends on how threatened I feel. I have learned to say I am sorry, pick up the phone when I have stepped on somebody's toes and try to make amends right away. I have too often seen the little stupid misunderstandings gone wild. It can destroy friendships and last over long periods of time. So, I am getting more and more direct. It's maybe a little uncomfortable at the moment, but it sure takes care of things. Directness and bluntness don't mean being hurtful. On the contrary, I am trying to be sincere and honest. Who wants to fight that? I wished I had known about this way of communicating when I had my fallout with my sister years ago. Now, so much time has passed, and it gets harder and harder. Who begins? And will I get hurt again?

I wished I could be that strong in all aspects of life. When I get really hurt, I tend to react in my old ways. Reaction instead of thinking is a bad thing. I have changed a lot over the years and the stronger more direct me is spilling over into my marriage and my life in general. My pleasing behaviors are losing their grip. Honesty, integrity and direct communications will always be the right way for me. I can't handle lies, cattiness and backstabbing in others. I don't want to use them myself. It's not who I want to be. I am not talking about the little fib we all use when asked if the dress gives your girlfriend a fat butt.

I learned as a child that I had to please everybody at all times. It has always interfered with my life. How do you stand up for yourself and please at the same time? I do please myself when I can stand up and be forceful without raising my voice and when I don't fall apart and cry. I please me when I can state my opinion in a non-threatening way. In the old days, I would have ended relationships over minor incidences because I didn't know how to act at all. I thought I had no say and everybody was out to get me. It's a huge change, and the world has become a lot easier to live in.

There are many reasons to love CoDA. There are meetings all over the country, meetings on many days a week if you need them and it also feels good to have found a place to go that doesn't cost anything. So, when therapy is over, there is a safe heaven, people to talk to and a camaraderie I had never known before. It's as if we have our own language. We have a very honest and open language and a way to talk to each other that you can't use with everybody in this world. Nothing is too sad to talk about, and no one judges you, and there is no gossip. It is a wonderful fellowship of people from all walks of life, sharing and wanting to heal. We are all learning to live life, instead of surviving life.

It is as if all the work I had done inside the therapy realm has to be done again out in the real world. Much of my old thinking patterns needed to be aired again and seen from another angle. It's very rewarding to be trusted and cared for by like-minded people.

It's so refreshing to have this kind of profound talking and sharing. I think we live in a world where people talk about television programs, sports and celebrities more than about who we are or what we think and feel. I think we have lost something and the texting and emailing haven't helped. I use them both, but picking up the phone and actually asking "How are you?" is very important for our emotional health. We live in a world where our looks are more important than our inner peace. I find that so sad.

From hating my first day at CoDA, I now can't wait to go to my weekly meeting.

I want my chip back.

SNIPPET THIRTY-ONE:
CHANGING AND FORGIVING

Where can the healing take me? That's a difficult question to answer. Is there an answer? I don't know. What I certainly do know is what progress feels like when I meet it. Here is a small example.

My bad or false self-image comes from my negative and unhappy feelings as a child. The messages I received from my parents became my reality, and I believed the lies that I was second-class and a nobody. I had learned to judge myself harshly and with negativity. I created a facade to survive in this world—an outer personality that was an imposter. I can explain it like this. The fake me and the feeling of being an imposter come from all the different faces I had to put on as I changed to mentally survive as a child. The faces didn't feel right in the moment. Over the years, I didn't like myself when I became chameleon-like to please others or to stay out of a confrontation or other trouble. What I have not been able to recognize is that all these faces or coping mechanisms have many talents and can be fun and happy. They are capable of a lot of stuff, and people enjoy being around me when I put on my fun and charming facade. But, it was never real to me. I thought I had to stay dumb and second-class. In essence, all my talents and my positive, happy faces belonged to the imposter. The real me had to hide from the world. No one could ever be allowed to see the flawed me.

Whenever I was given a compliment, I wouldn't hear it, or I thought that the compliment was meant for the imposter...the fake me who had all the fun. This became real to me only when one woman in group therapy asked the following questions. "Do you only believe that compliments belong to your imposter?" "How can you ever heal if you can't see that you are both?" "Are you a combination of your past and the capable woman of today?" "Would it have been possible for you to act in these capable ways if you didn't have the means to do so already inside you?" Why hadn't I seen this before? It sounds so easy that it's absurd. In hiding my flawed self to the world, I had hidden the good side of me from myself. It's like a small miracle. No more feeling of being an imposter but better yet, I am now allowed to see myself as equal to everybody else. It's an awesome feeling. It's as if an empty spot near my heart is welling over with joy. I love it.

Sometimes progress is very slow, and other times it's so fast it takes my breath away.

In the future, I would love to be able to really and truly integrate all my faces and learn to be proud of who I am. I would love not hiding anything, not having to do everything in a hurry and not have to justify my every move. I would love to feel totally free to have my own opinions and feelings regardless of what other people think or feel.

I love when it happens...the respectful disagreement, the one with love for someone else's feelings, thoughts, emotions and opinions, with no resentment in any direction. I love it when no one is trying to control anybody else, just let other people have their feelings, just like you are having your feelings. No more statements like: you are wrong; you have the wrong opinion; you shouldn't speak, feel or think the way you do. I would like my future relationships to be in mutual respect and in acceptance that we aren't all the same and we learn to disagree with no bad feelings.

Coming to terms with my parents has taken a long time. They are both dead now, but their opinions of me still count, especially on bad and stressful days. I often ask myself if I harbor anger, hate and resentment towards them. I used to have an enmeshed love/hate relationship with them but, over the years, my feelings have calmed down a lot, and I don't hate them. There are days I miss them. I look back and think of them as two sad and overwhelmed people. It's a shame that so much damage was done by unthinking parents who never stopped to ask questions about their own lives or never thought anything could ever change. As my father once said to me, "I only had one pair of trousers growing up. That was enough for me, so it should be enough for my children." He didn't want better...it's so sad.

There is no doubt in my mind that my parents grew up in *The Soup*. And, as you know, *The Soup* is made of strong stuff. I almost copied them and could easily have relived their sad and unhappy lives. If I hadn't come out from under *The Fog* and seen the real world with its opportunities, I would have drowned and stayed depressed, just like so many women in the generations before me. I am almost out of *The Soup*. I hope by unloading all this pent-up energy and stale emotions into this book, I can stop hiding myself and let the naturally "happy me" be present all the time. I might even be able to sleep in a more normal way. As my wonderful daughter-in-law said one day, "If you could solve your sleep problems, you would be good to go."

I don't remember the exact number of years that I didn't have a relationship with my mother but probably around 15 or 16. I saw her a few times during that period—once at my father's funeral and once at a confirmation. We exchanged Christmas cards, and that was the only contact we had. She still had influence over my life even though I didn't see her. Every year when her Christmas card arrived in the mail, my inner children would quiver. Just her handwriting could make my system go haywire. My small girls were still needy for her and scared of her at the same time. My brother kept me posted, so I knew what was going on in her life. I often felt bad about staying silently away.

About four years ago, my husband and I had a conversation about my mother. He thought it would be a good idea for me to go and visit my now aging mother. He was afraid that the guilt in me would see no ending if she died before I had made some kind of peace with her. It would also be good to try out my new strong core up against my mother—to see if I would crumble or not. It was hard to pick up the phone and actually call her. The whole flock of girls was inside me waiting in anticipation of what was going to happen. Would she reject us? Would she be pleased to hear from us? She was very surprised to hear from me but also very happy. I told her I would come for afternoon tea.

She had moved into a little but cute home in a nice community for older folks. When I arrived, I was very guarded. I also felt strong. *I can handle this.* We spent the afternoon in her tiny, lovely garden. We had some good conversations, but maybe not as deep as I would have liked them to be. I had to realize that I had gone through therapy and lived abroad and that she had pretty much lived the same way as always. We spoke to each other as adults, and she never treated me as her small little girl. If she had, I would have left, and I think she sensed that. We were talking a lot about her life after my father's death. She told me that even though she missed him, she had finally found some part of herself that had been missing for years. She had finally been able and allowed to make decisions for herself. No one was belittling her and telling her what to do. She had tears in her eyes when she told me how freeing it was to be able to furnish her own place and not have to cook dinner unless you want to cook. She could even stay out all day with her friends. She had made many new friends, and I felt she was happy. Better late than never!

I felt happy for her. She was no longer a threat to my inner girls. My husband had been very wise in suggesting that I go to see her. I visited her one more afternoon in her little garden before she died. I am glad that I did get to see her one more time. I hope she is in a peaceful and loving place some-where. She did not have an easy life. Actually, at my father's funeral, I wrote the same words on the little card I had attached to the flowers I had brought. "I wish you will find a loving and peaceful place, somewhere nice." Sometimes I miss him too. I have never grieved his death because I was so angry. Perhaps one day I will get to that.

In writing these words about my parents, I can feel I have come a long way, and much of my old anger and sadness are gone. If I stayed angry and hated my parents that was equal to staying in *The Soup* and I know that is a bad place. I never thought it would be possible for me to forgive my parents. Today I can honestly say and write, "I forgive you both." It has been many years since the healer in Switzerland told me to do exactly that.

I hereby set myself free from any bad feelings festering inside me. It feels good. I ask myself if I could have forgiven them that day in the little chapel in Switzerland. Did I really have to go through all that hard work? There is a part of me that wishes it could have been easier but just saying the words "I forgive" doesn't cut it. I have to really mean it in my heart.

NOT KNOWING WHERE
TO GO FROM HERE:

Shortly after I had finished writing my story, I began to wonder what to do with it all. I spent weeks of reflecting upon my writing and why I had done it.

First, I began to write merely because I couldn't stop. While I was writing, a little hope began to emerge. Maybe this could become a book. I was writing whatever came to my mind. I didn't outline or have notes. Frankly, I had no idea what I was doing. It poured out of me in raw spurts of emotion. It came straight from the heart, and slowly my feelings began to show themselves on the paper. I would find a comfy chair and start writing in my horrible handwriting. It just kept coming page after page. I tried not to censor myself too much and write my thoughts as they came to me. It was almost like the book was already inside me—it just needed to physically get onto paper. Sometimes too many thoughts and memories flooded over me at the same time and I would look up to the heavens and ask, "Could you hold that thought for me...please?" This also worked when some overwhelming thought came to me while driving. I would send it away to be held for me so that I could continue driving in safety.

It was overwhelming to even think of publishing, but I knew it would feel great to be able to stand tall and have my voice heard. I would feel that I had accomplished something in my life. Of course, doubts began to creep in, and the old voices were there too. *You think you are an author?* And the usual chatter of denial followed me around. *What will people think of me?*

I wanted it out there for many reasons. I was hoping I could gain some strength from letting it all out—a form of cleansing. I was also hoping that some struggling soul could gain something from my honesty. I do believe that a lot of people are afraid of sharing their innermost feelings, and, in some cases, rightfully so. I always thought that if people knew of my depression and sadness, they would dislike and reject me. I also believed that any knowledge of me could be used to hurt me again and again. Then I would be back in a lonely place. The old message was still inside me.

So, letting somebody actually read my story was nerve racking for me.

I didn't know what to do about it all and left it to my *H*igher *P*ower—if this was going to be a book, *HP* would help me. Shortly after I had that thought, it became my turn to choose a book for my monthly book club. *Maybe I should give them my first draft and see what happens?* I played with that thought a while. I wasn't sure. After a couple of weeks, I had gathered enough strength to go ahead with it. I made eight copies and handed them out. I felt very vulnerable, and my inner children weren't happy with me.

Then came the wait. I was hoping I didn't have to wait a whole month before somebody would come back to me with a reaction. After about a week, I received a long and remarkable letter. It not only thanked me for daring to be so open and honest but also told a story about someone else's childhood sadness that I would otherwise not have known. Then other letters and emails arrived, and the same was repeated. I couldn't have been happier. No one was rejecting me—instead, they trusted me with their stories. Once again, my old beliefs were wrong. I felt I became a better friend and I felt a lot closer to these women than before.

When I dared open up for old wounds, so did they. At the book club meeting that next month, we spoke to each other in a new fashion. We had the longest meeting ever, and I loved every minute of it…because sharing is always healing.

It was the first time in my life that I had been totally honest about my sadness and depression, except in individual or group therapy or with trusted old girlfriends. It felt very liberating. Here, in my new country, I can allow myself to be free and truthful with myself and others. I didn't have to lie by omission…trying to pretend I grew up in a big happy family.

Then I met a lovely woman named Joan. We were talking about what we were doing in life. I told her I was writing a book about my life. "Do you want me to edit it for you?" she asked. I couldn't believe my ears. What is the chance to meet a person who does this kind of work—at the exact moment you need it? We hardly knew each other when I handed my draft to her. I was again both scared and happy. I instinctively knew she would have respect for my emotions and that she wouldn't change my way of saying things. She called almost daily with questions and wanted to get to know me better, just as I wanted to get to know her better. After some weeks, she had read it over a couple of times, and we met for lunch. I could hardly wait to hear what she had to say. I was like a small child with butterflies in my stomach. She liked it and began working on it soon after. Happy again. She asked me questions about how and where to publish.

The book became a little more real in my mind. This was very scary to my inner children.

As I was driving home, my inner children were running amok. *If you ever talk about it all, you will have to die.* It went on and on. The childhood beliefs were still insisting that I was putting myself in danger. I tried to push it all away, but as soon as I got home, I crashed.

It had been years since the feeling of imminent doom had surfaced like it did that day. I stood in my kitchen shaking, tears of fear and sadness came rolling down, and I began to pace around the house. I couldn't relax at all. I tried to make myself a cup of tea but never managed it. I was doing the forbidden, and I had to be punished. A part of me wanted to throw away every single written page.

I don't remember how long I paced around before my husband entered the house. I told him what was up and he helped me calm down. We were both shocked! We had been convinced that my new inner strength could cope with anything. Of course, I was scared about sharing my writings with the world. I was scared. It was surprising that it could bring me down like that. I didn't feel good the rest of the day, and I didn't sleep a lot that night. The next day I felt I was back in the saddle again. It never ceases to amaze me how forceful and powerful the early programming can be. It is a constant dialog between the new and the old ways of thinking. When too much stress is present, the old patterns can take over, even after so many years of healing.

This little setback made me think about how far I had come since the lifting of *The Fog* when I was around 20-years-old. When I look back and see the unhappy person, I can fully appreciate how far I have come. It is like I have had several lives. I look back and mourn for my little, scared girl and my depressed woman. I think I had to write this book to honor them. I didn't want their sufferings to be in vain. I couldn't bear it if my inner voices weren't ever heard. For many years, I didn't want to hear them. Then, I slowly began to hear, but I didn't want to believe. In a weird way, I rejected my inner children the same way I was fearing people would reject me.

So again, I am asking my *Higher Power*, "Let's see where this book will take me?"

Otherwise, there is nothing left to say except thanks to everybody who helped me. Thanks to the readers for picking up this book. I hope it will help you in your way to healing.

Everything is possible…

LAST LITTLE SNIPPET:

I have always listened to the saying, "Do unto others as you would have them do unto you." That is all good, but someone turned it around, and I absolutely love it. "Learn to love and treat yourself as kindly as you treat others." Personally, it makes a lot of sense. I never speak to people in the bad way that I speak to myself. I never allow myself to let people down like I would for myself. I will continue to make an effort to treat myself as an invited honored guest.

Over the years, I have met some wonderful people, both healing professionals and caring friends. This book could not have been written without them, my Higher Power, my ever supporting husband and my angels. Thanks to you all.

The End

Made in the USA
San Bernardino, CA
20 May 2017